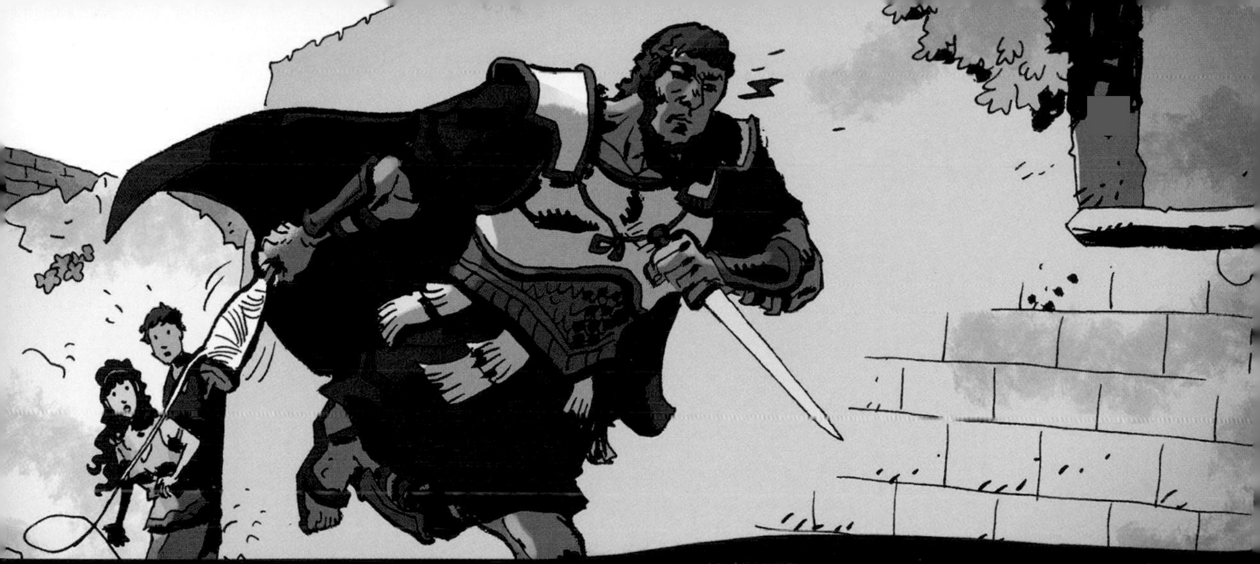

THESEUS AND THE MINOTAUR

A GRAPHIC RETELLING

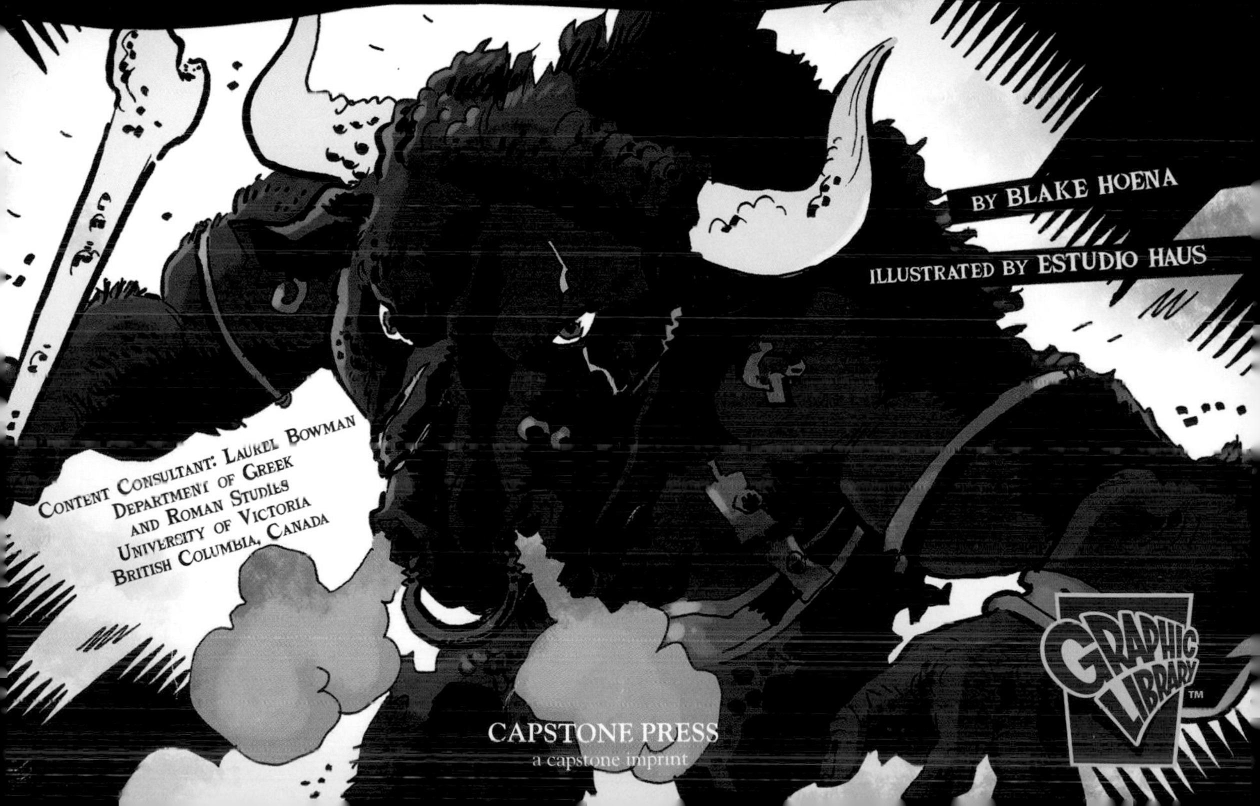

BY BLAKE HOENA

ILLUSTRATED BY ESTUDIO HAUS

CONTENT CONSULTANT: LAUREL BOWMAN
DEPARTMENT OF GREEK
AND ROMAN STUDIES
UNIVERSITY OF VICTORIA
BRITISH COLUMBIA, CANADA

GRAPHIC LIBRARY™

CAPSTONE PRESS
a capstone imprint

Graphic Library is published by Capstone Press,
1710 Roe Crest Drive, North Mankato, Minnesota 56003
www.capstonepub.com

Library of Congress Cataloging-in-Publication Data
Hoena, B. A., author.
  Theseus and the Minotaur : a graphic retelling / by Blake Hoena ; illustrated by Estudio Haus.
      pages cm.—(Graphic library. Ancient myths.)
  Summary:"The story of Theseus and his quest to defeat the Minotaur in the labyrinth told in
graphic novel format"—Provided by publisher.
  Audience: Ages 8-14.
  Audience: Grades 4 to 6.
  Includes bibliographical references and index.
  ISBN 978-1-4914-2075-1 (library binding)
  ISBN 978-1-4914-2279-3 (paperback)
  ISBN 978-1-4914-2293-9 (eBook pdf)
1. Theseus (Greek mythology)—Comic books, strips, etc. 2. Theseus (Greek mythology)—Juvenile
literature. 3. Minotaur (Greek mythology)—Comic books, strips, etc. 4. Minotaur (Greek
mythology)—Juvenile literature. 5. Mythology, Greek—Comic books, strips, etc. 6. Mythology,
Greek—Juvenile literature. I. Estudio Haus (Firm), illustrator. II. Title.
  BL820.T5H64 2015
  398.2'0938—dc23   2014019196

Editor
Anthony Wacholtz

Art Director
Nathan Gassman

Designer
Ashlee Suker

Production Specialist
Tori Abraham

Printed in the United States of America in
Stevens Point, Wisconsin
092014   008479WZS15

TABLE OF CONTENTS

ORIGINS OF THE MYTH

Apollodorus (180 BC–120 BC) was a Greek historian and scholar. This adaptation of Theseus' story is based largely on his book *The Library*. Apollodorus' book includes many ancient myths, including the 12 labors of Hercules.

CHAPTER ONE
YOUNG THESEUS

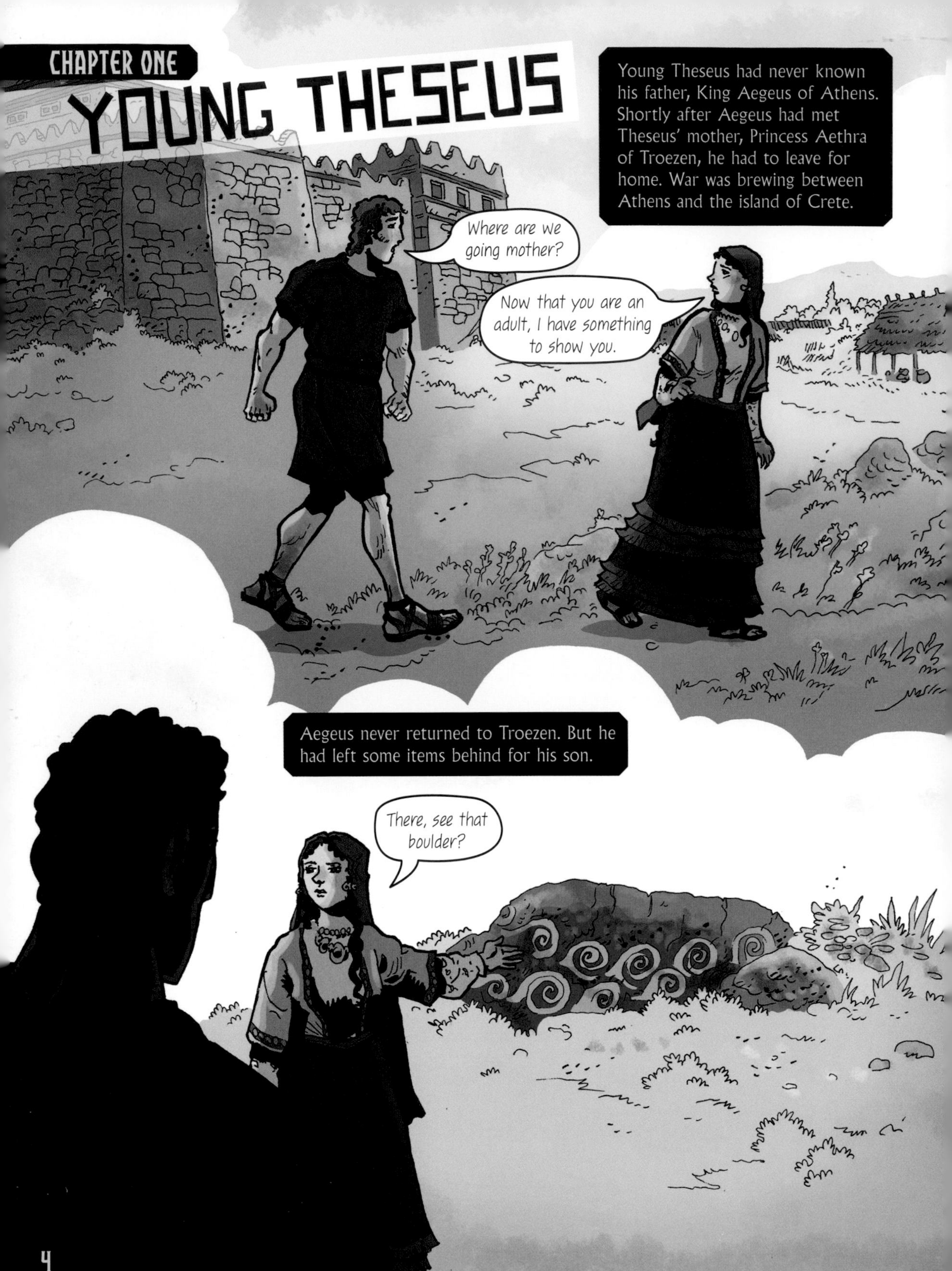
Young Theseus had never known his father, King Aegeus of Athens. Shortly after Aegeus had met Theseus' mother, Princess Aethra of Troezen, he had to leave for home. War was brewing between Athens and the island of Crete.
Where are we going mother?
Now that you are an adult, I have something to show you.
Aegeus never returned to Troezen. But he had left some items behind for his son.
There, see that boulder?

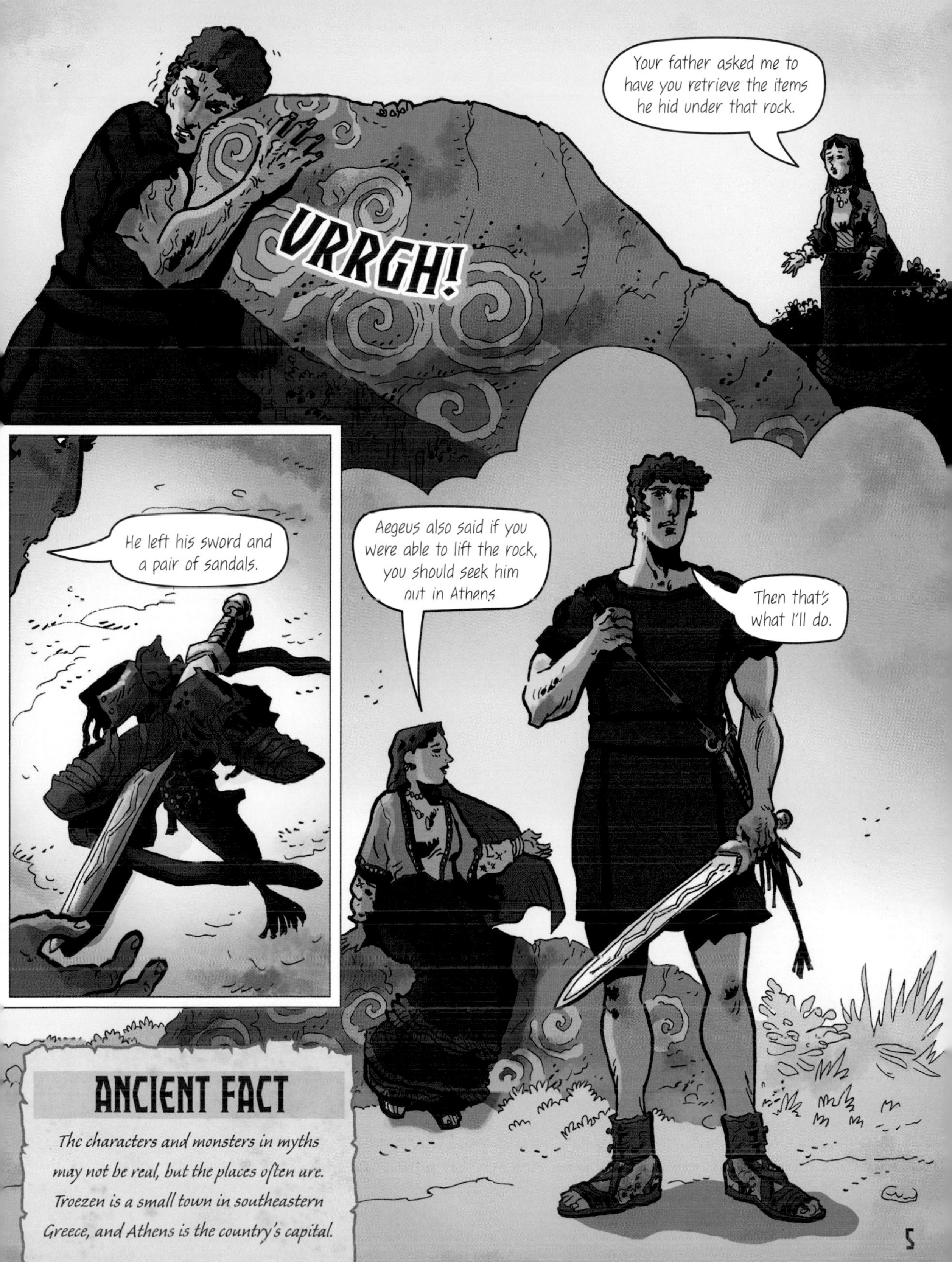
Your father asked me to have you retrieve the items he hid under that rock.
URRGH!
He left his sword and a pair of sandals.
Aegeus also said if you were able to lift the rock, you should seek him out in Athens.
Then that's what I'll do.

ANCIENT FACT

The characters and monsters in myths may not be real, but the places often are. Troezen is a small town in southeastern Greece, and Athens is the country's capital.

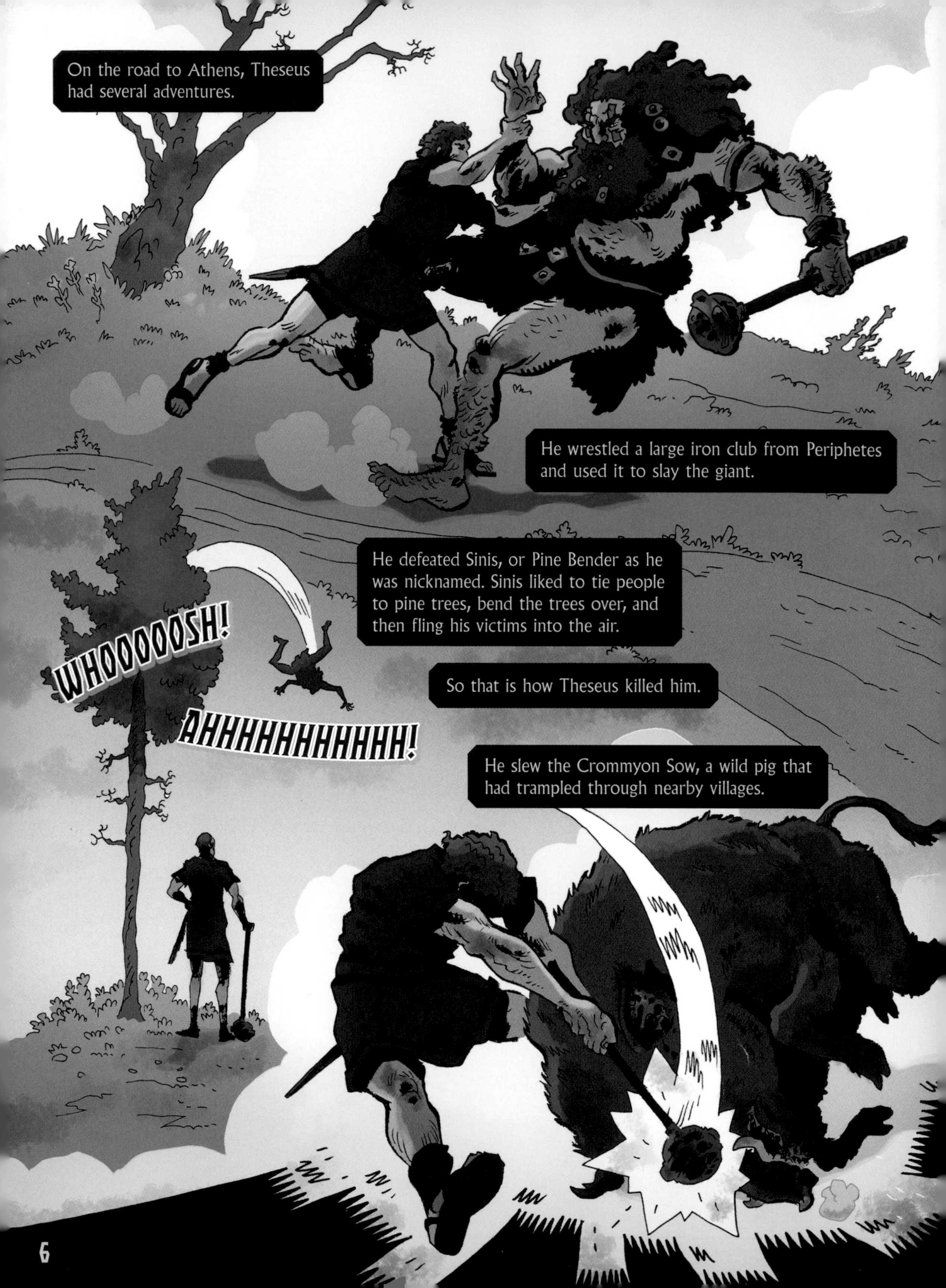
On the road to Athens, Theseus had several adventures.
He wrestled a large iron club from Periphetes and used it to slay the giant.
He defeated Sinis, or Pine Bender as he was nicknamed. Sinis liked to tie people to pine trees, bend the trees over, and then fling his victims into the air.
WHOOOOOOSH!
AHHHHHHHHHHH!
So that is how Theseus killed him.
He slew the Crommyon Sow, a wild pig that had trampled through nearby villages.

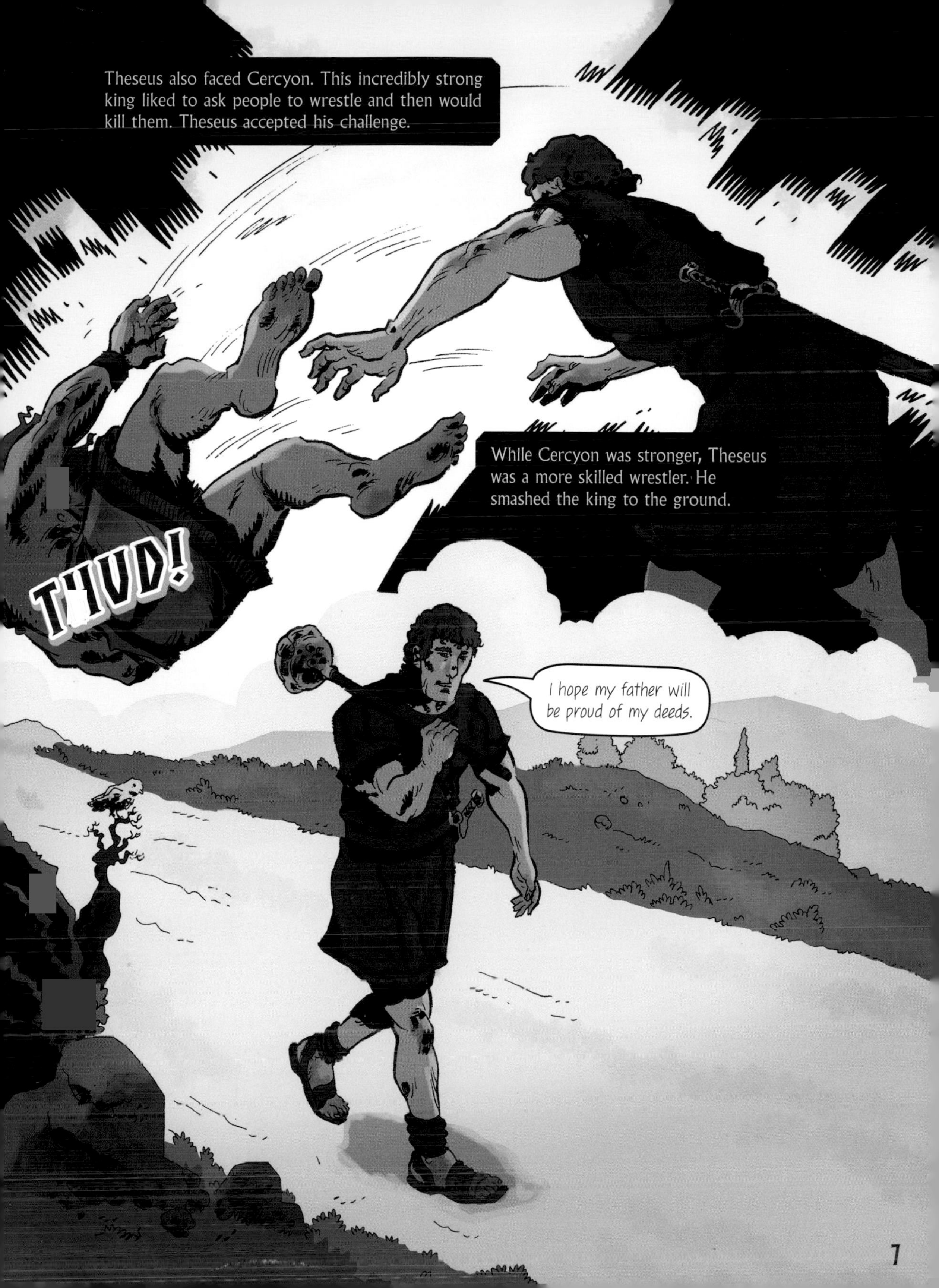
Theseus also faced Cercyon. This incredibly strong king liked to ask people to wrestle and then would kill them. Theseus accepted his challenge.
While Cercyon was stronger, Theseus was a more skilled wrestler. He smashed the king to the ground.
THUD!
I hope my father will be proud of my deeds.

CHAPTER TWO

ATHENS

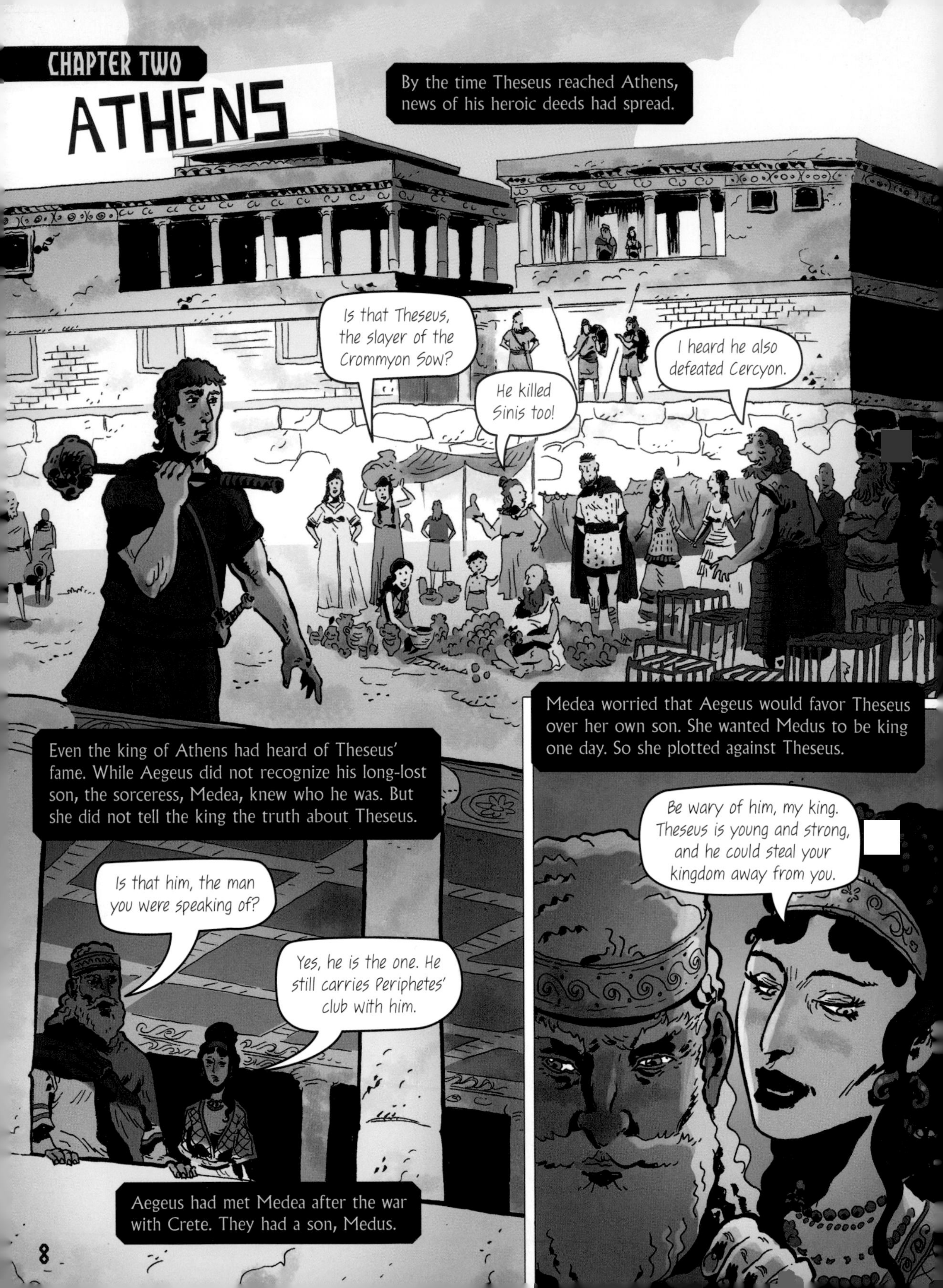
By the time Theseus reached Athens, news of his heroic deeds had spread.
Is that Theseus, the slayer of the Crommyon Sow?
He killed Sinis too!
I heard he also defeated Cercyon.
Even the king of Athens had heard of Theseus' fame. While Aegeus did not recognize his long-lost son, the sorceress, Medea, knew who he was. But she did not tell the king the truth about Theseus.
Is that him, the man you were speaking of?
Yes, he is the one. He still carries Periphetes' club with him.
Aegeus had met Medea after the war with Crete. They had a son, Medus.
Medea worried that Aegeus would favor Theseus over her own son. She wanted Medus to be king one day. So she plotted against Theseus.
Be wary of him, my king. Theseus is young and strong, and he could steal your kingdom away from you.

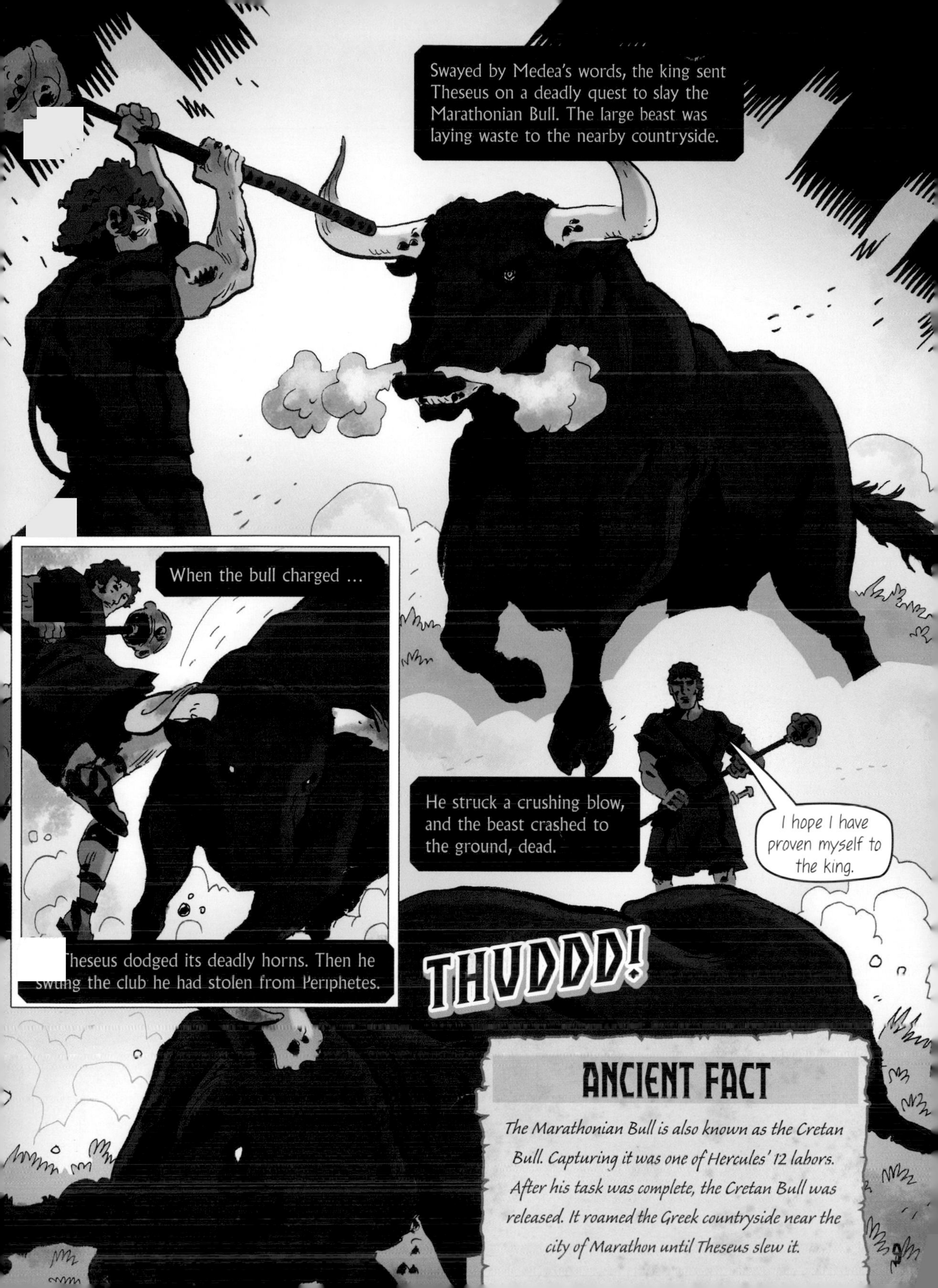
Swayed by Medea's words, the king sent Theseus on a deadly quest to slay the Marathonian Bull. The large beast was laying waste to the nearby countryside.
When the bull charged ...
Theseus dodged its deadly horns. Then he swung the club he had stolen from Periphetes.
THUDDD!
He struck a crushing blow, and the beast crashed to the ground, dead.
I hope I have proven myself to the king.
ANCIENT FACT
The Marathonian Bull is also known as the Cretan Bull. Capturing it was one of Hercules' 12 labors. After his task was complete, the Cretan Bull was released. It roamed the Greek countryside near the city of Marathon until Theseus slew it.

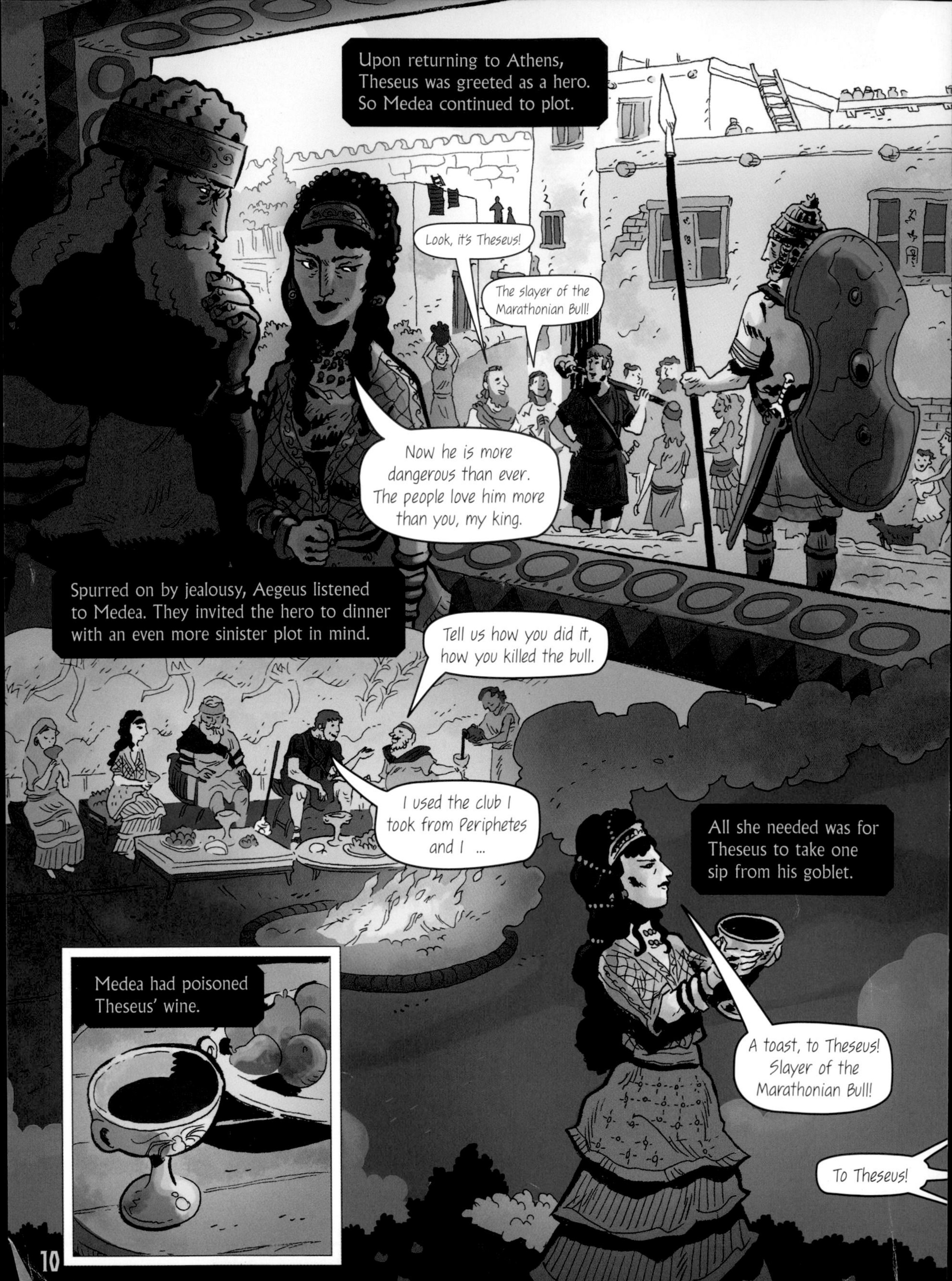
Upon returning to Athens, Theseus was greeted as a hero. So Medea continued to plot.
Look, it's Theseus!
The slayer of the Marathonian Bull!
Now he is more dangerous than ever. The people love him more than you, my king.
Spurred on by jealousy, Aegeus listened to Medea. They invited the hero to dinner with an even more sinister plot in mind.
Tell us how you did it, how you killed the bull.
I used the club I took from Periphetes and I ...
All she needed was for Theseus to take one sip from his goblet.
Medea had poisoned Theseus' wine.
A toast, to Theseus! Slayer of the Marathonian Bull!
To Theseus!

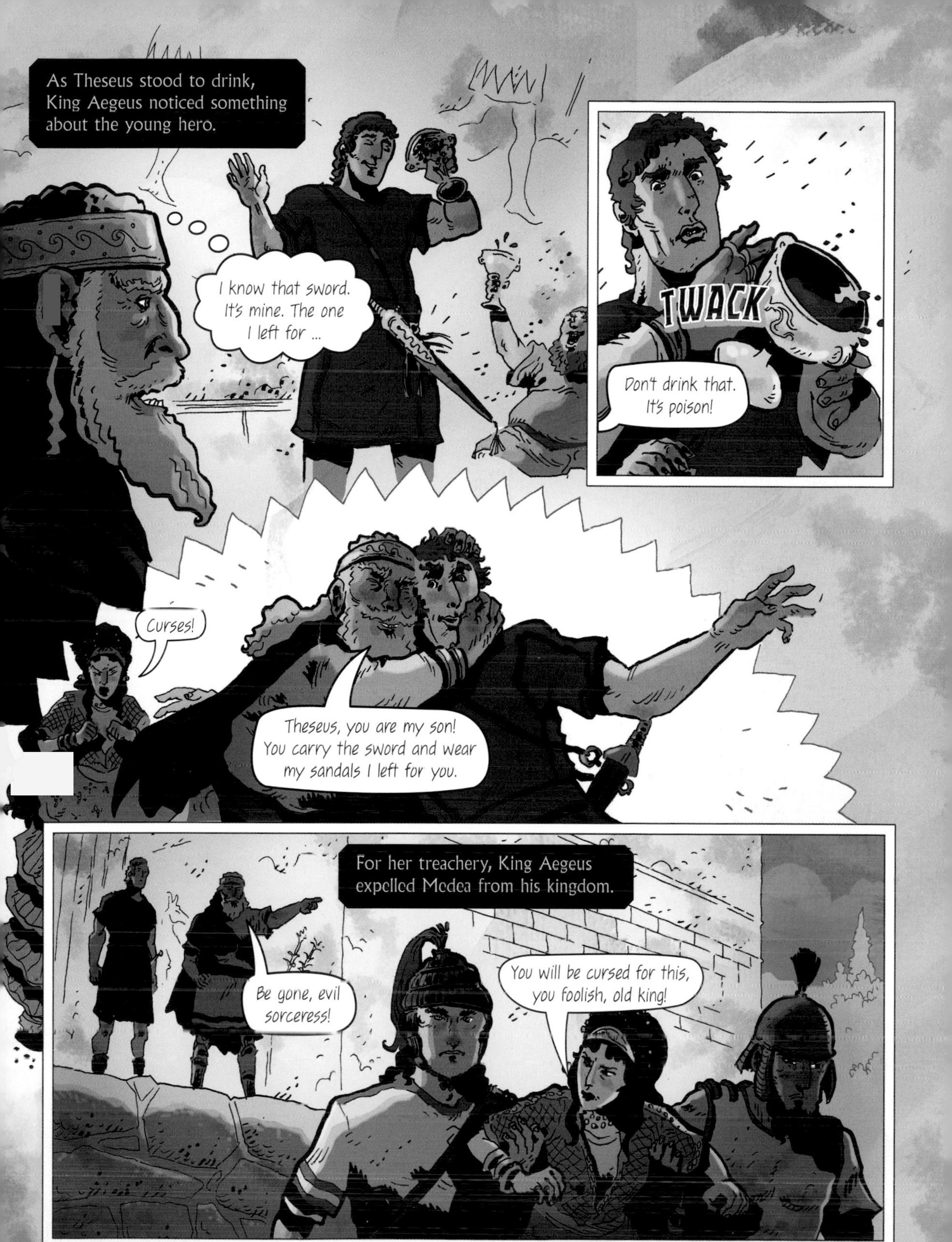
As Theseus stood to drink, King Aegeus noticed something about the young hero.
I know that sword. It's mine. The one I left for ...
TWACK
Don't drink that. It's poison!
Curses!
Theseus, you are my son! You carry the sword and wear my sandals I left for you.
For her treachery, King Aegeus expelled Medea from his kingdom.
Be gone, evil sorceress!
You will be cursed for this, you foolish, old king!

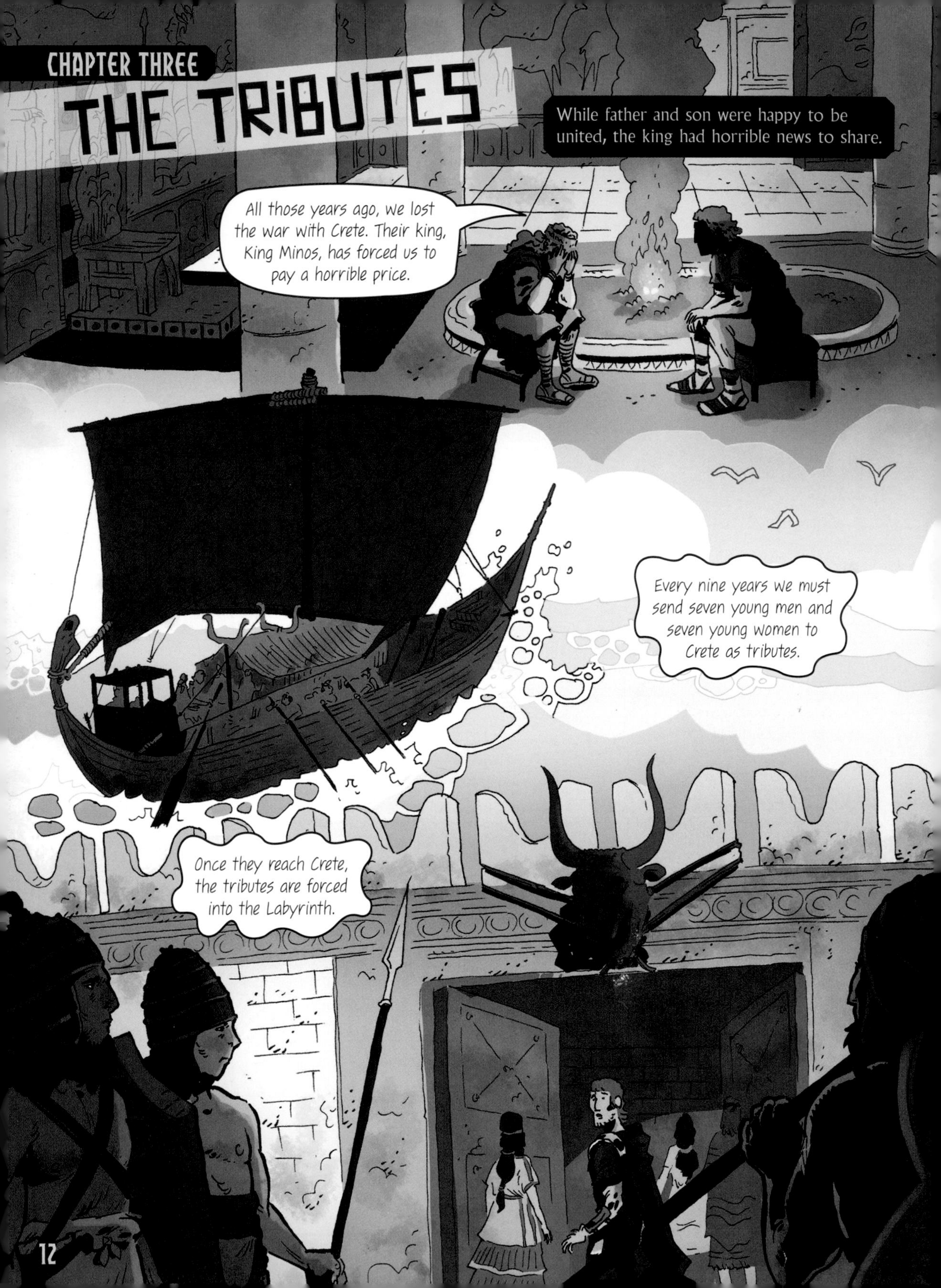
CHAPTER THREE
THE TRIBUTES
While father and son were happy to be united, the king had horrible news to share.
All those years ago, we lost the war with Crete. Their king, King Minos, has forced us to pay a horrible price.
Every nine years we must send seven young men and seven young women to Crete as tributes.
Once they reach Crete, the tributes are forced into the Labyrinth.

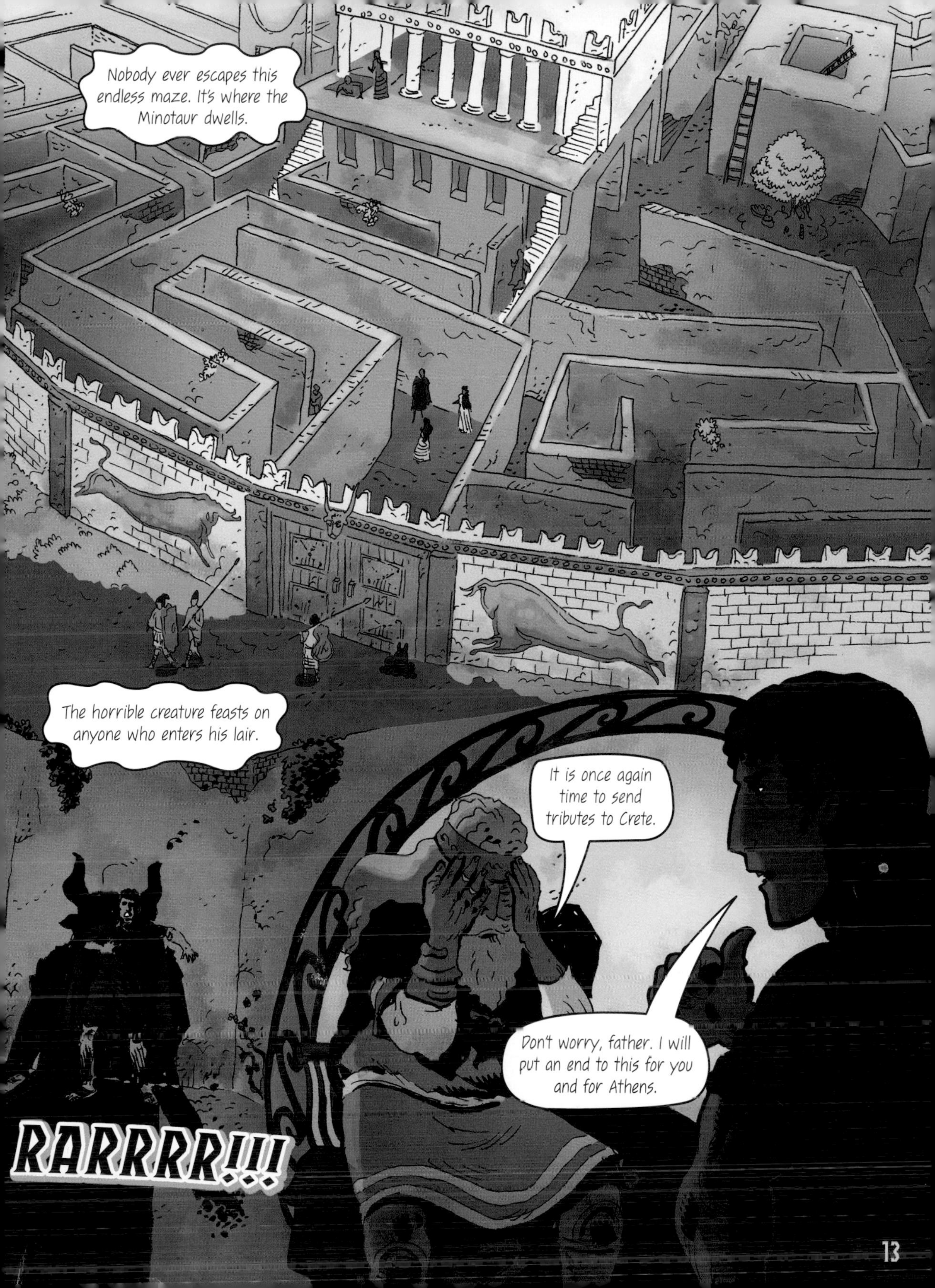
Nobody ever escapes this endless maze. It's where the Minotaur dwells.
The horrible creature feasts on anyone who enters his lair.
RARRRRR!!!
It is once again time to send tributes to Crete.
Don't worry, father. I will put an end to this for you and for Athens.

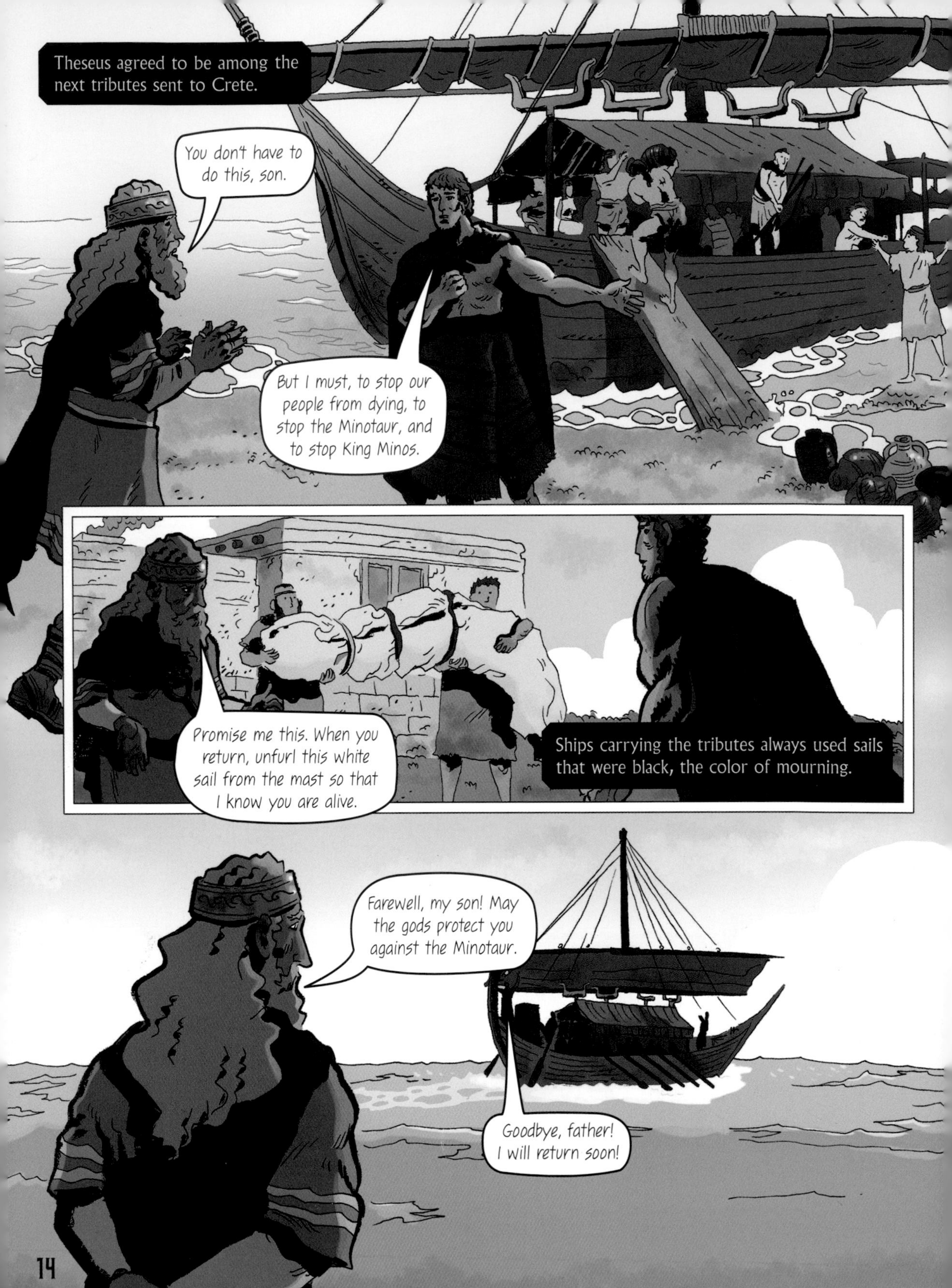
Theseus agreed to be among the next tributes sent to Crete.
You don't have to do this, son.
But I must, to stop our people from dying, to stop the Minotaur, and to stop King Minos.
Promise me this. When you return, unfurl this white sail from the mast so that I know you are alive.
Ships carrying the tributes always used sails that were black, the color of mourning.
Farewell, my son! May the gods protect you against the Minotaur.
Goodbye, father! I will return soon!

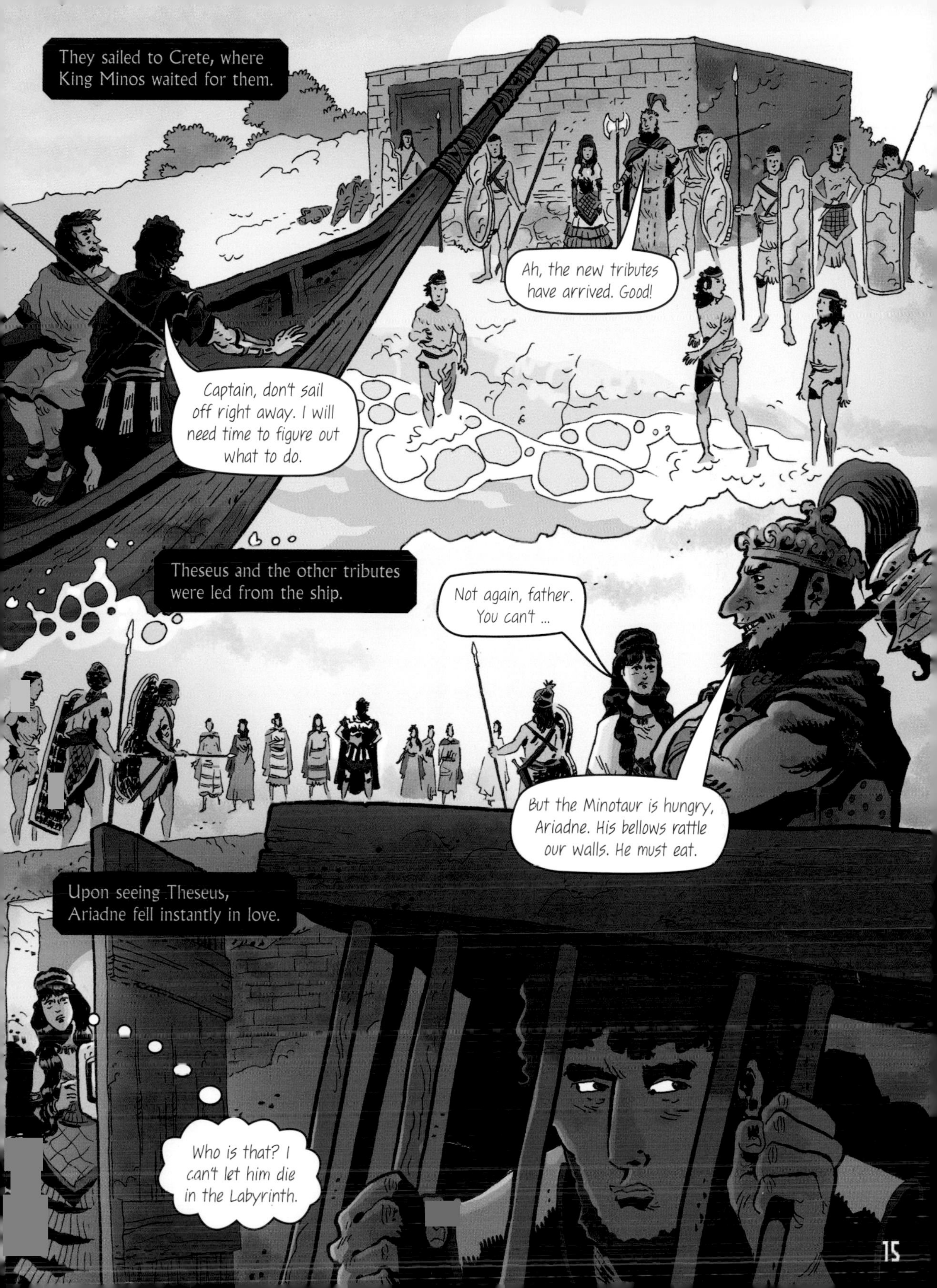
They sailed to Crete, where King Minos waited for them.
Ah, the new tributes have arrived. Good!
Captain, don't sail off right away. I will need time to figure out what to do.
Theseus and the other tributes were led from the ship.
Not again, father. You can't ...
But the Minotaur is hungry, Ariadne. His bellows rattle our walls. He must eat.
Upon seeing Theseus, Ariadne fell instantly in love.
Who is that? I can't let him die in the Labyrinth.

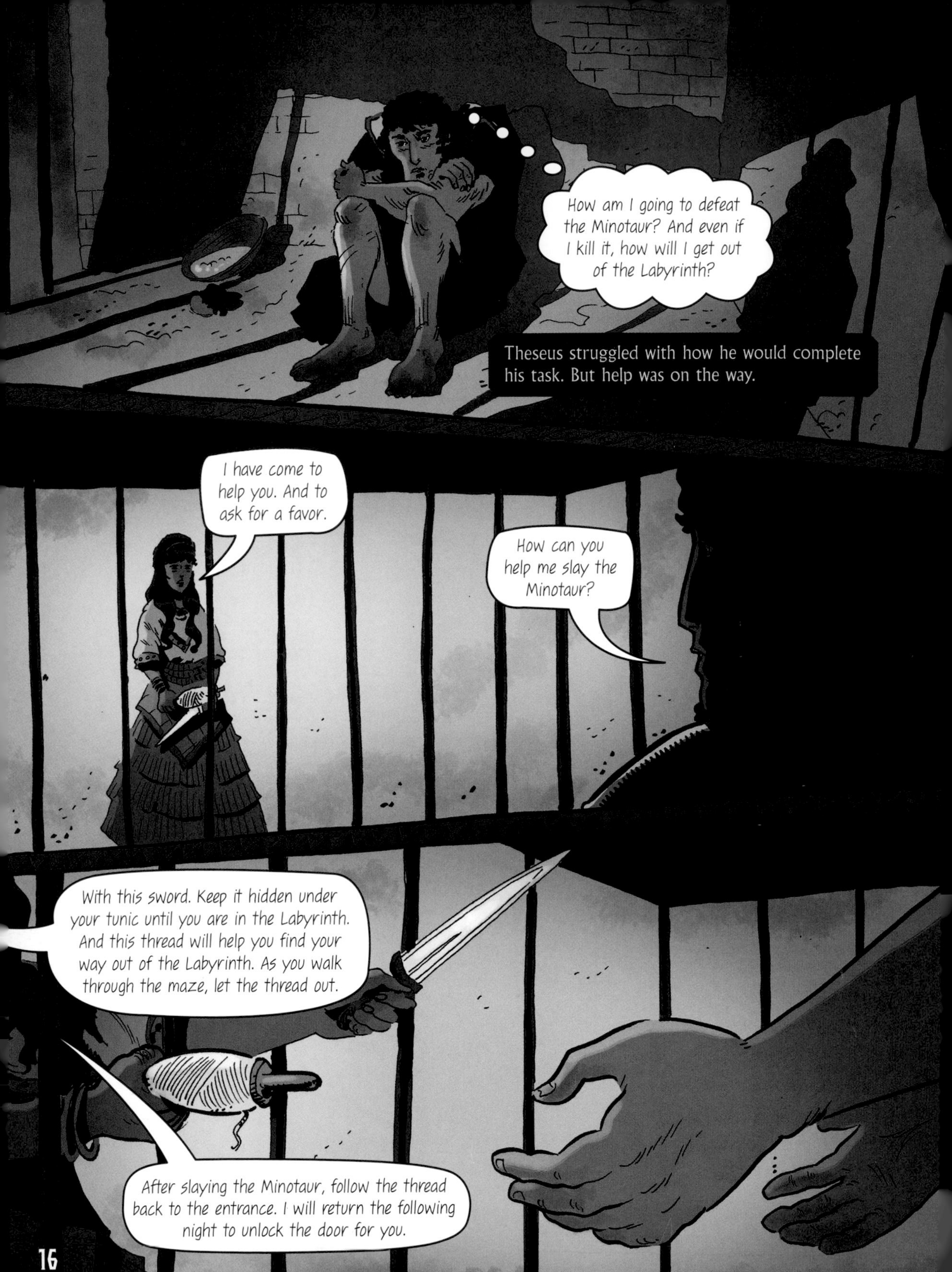
How am I going to defeat the Minotaur? And even if I kill it, how will I get out of the Labyrinth?
Theseus struggled with how he would complete his task. But help was on the way.
I have come to help you. And to ask for a favor.
How can you help me slay the Minotaur?
With this sword. Keep it hidden under your tunic until you are in the Labyrinth. And this thread will help you find your way out of the Labyrinth. As you walk through the maze, let the thread out.
After slaying the Minotaur, follow the thread back to the entrance. I will return the following night to unlock the door for you.

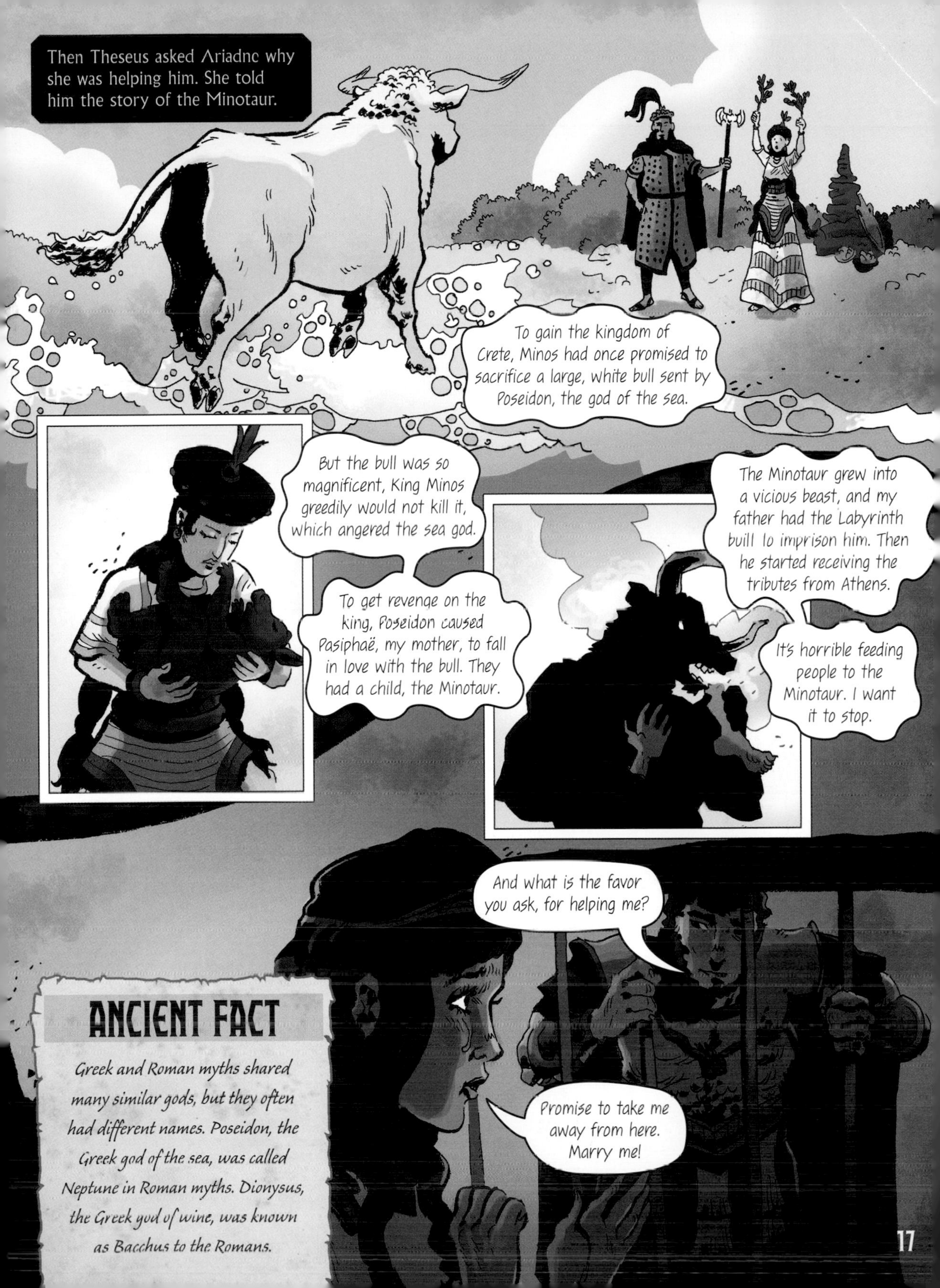
Then Theseus asked Ariadne why she was helping him. She told him the story of the Minotaur.
To gain the kingdom of Crete, Minos had once promised to sacrifice a large, white bull sent by Poseidon, the god of the sea.
But the bull was so magnificent, King Minos greedily would not kill it, which angered the sea god.
To get revenge on the king, Poseidon caused Pasiphaë, my mother, to fall in love with the bull. They had a child, the Minotaur.
The Minotaur grew into a vicious beast, and my father had the Labyrinth built to imprison him. Then he started receiving the tributes from Athens.
It's horrible feeding people to the Minotaur. I want it to stop.
And what is the favor you ask, for helping me?
Promise to take me away from here. Marry me!

ANCIENT FACT

Greek and Roman myths shared many similar gods, but they often had different names. Poseidon, the Greek god of the sea, was called Neptune in Roman myths. Dionysus, the Greek god of wine, was known as Bacchus to the Romans.

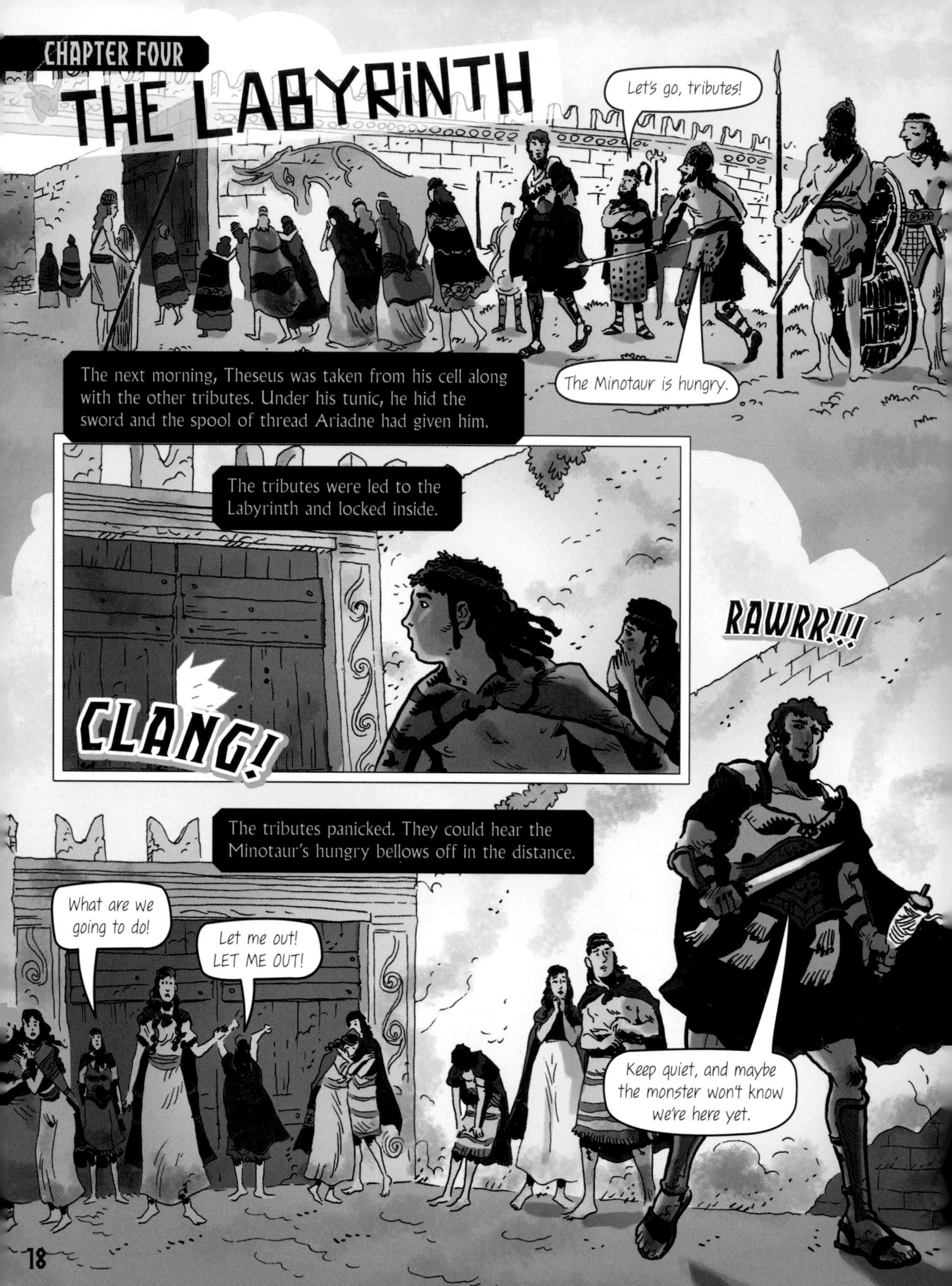
CHAPTER FOUR
THE LABYRINTH
Let's go, tributes!
The next morning, Theseus was taken from his cell along with the other tributes. Under his tunic, he hid the sword and the spool of thread Ariadne had given him.
The Minotaur is hungry.
The tributes were led to the Labyrinth and locked inside.
CLANG!
RAWRR!!!
The tributes panicked. They could hear the Minotaur's hungry bellows off in the distance.
What are we going to do!
Let me out! LET ME OUT!
Keep quiet, and maybe the monster won't know we're here yet.

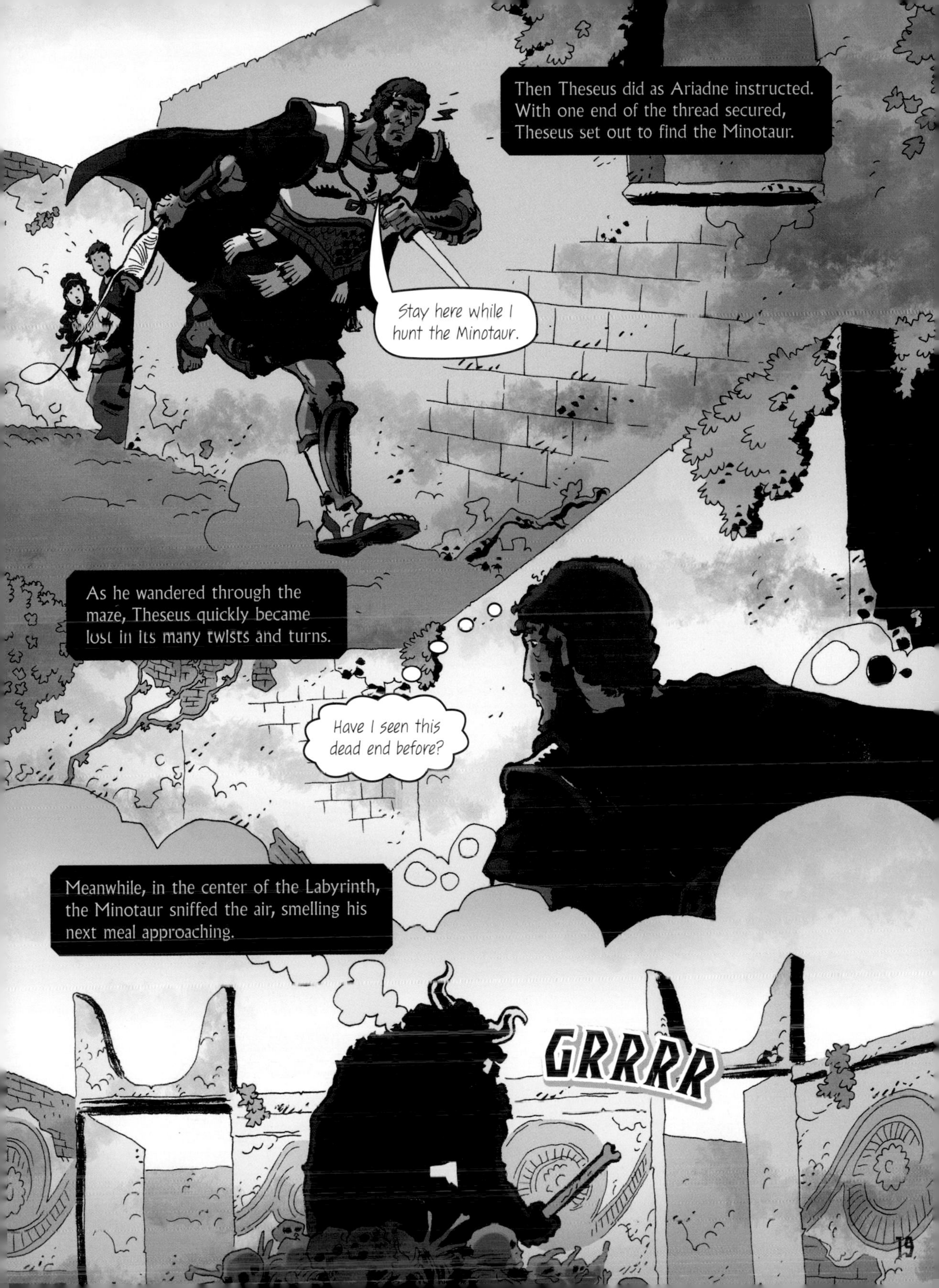

Then Theseus did as Ariadne instructed. With one end of the thread secured, Theseus set out to find the Minotaur.
Stay here while I hunt the Minotaur.
As he wandered through the maze, Theseus quickly became lost in its many twists and turns.
Have I seen this dead end before?
Meanwhile, in the center of the Labyrinth, the Minotaur sniffed the air, smelling his next meal approaching.
GRRRR

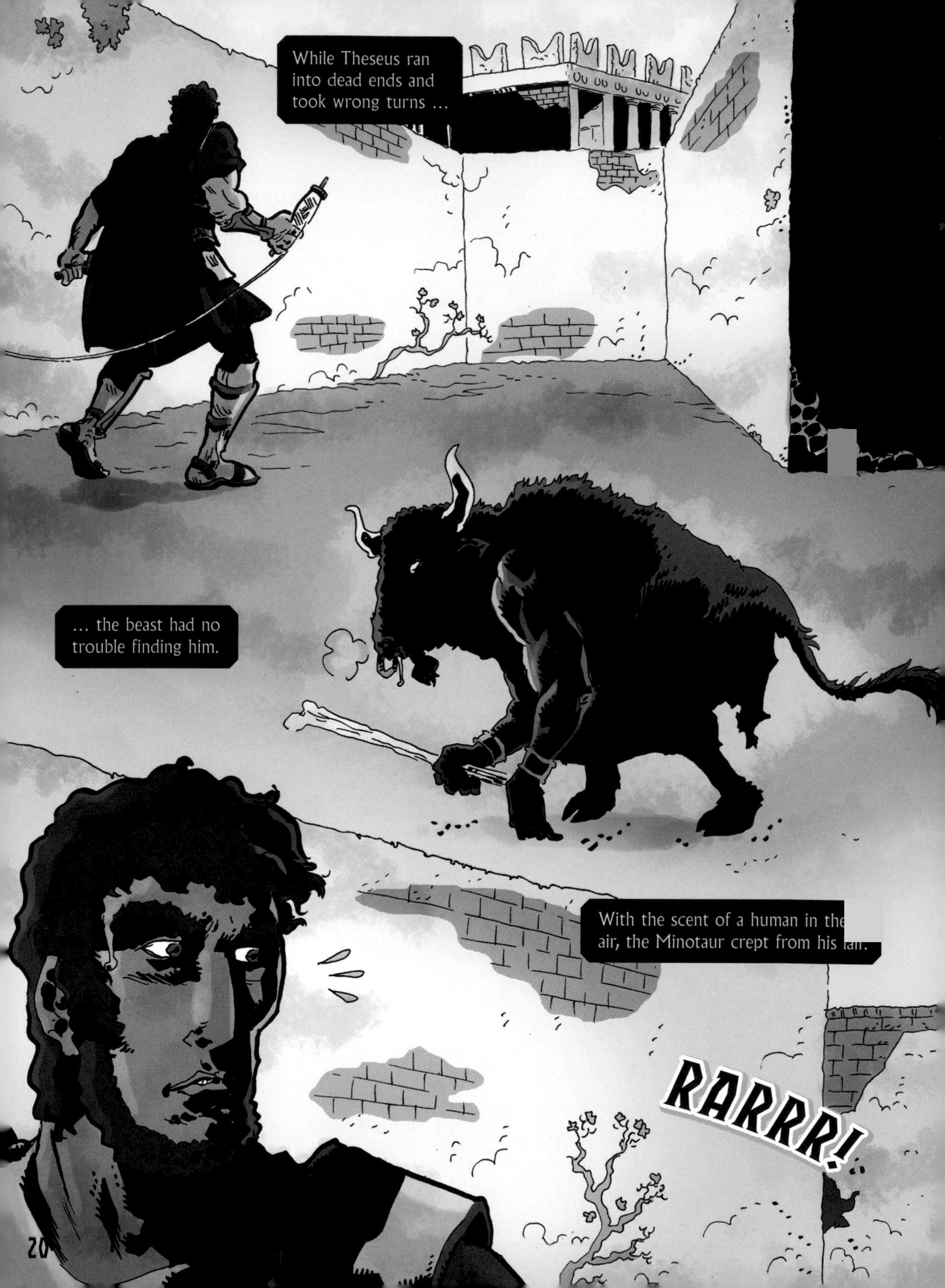
While Theseus ran into dead ends and took wrong turns ...
... the beast had no trouble finding him.
With the scent of a human in the
air, the Minotaur crept from his
RARRR!

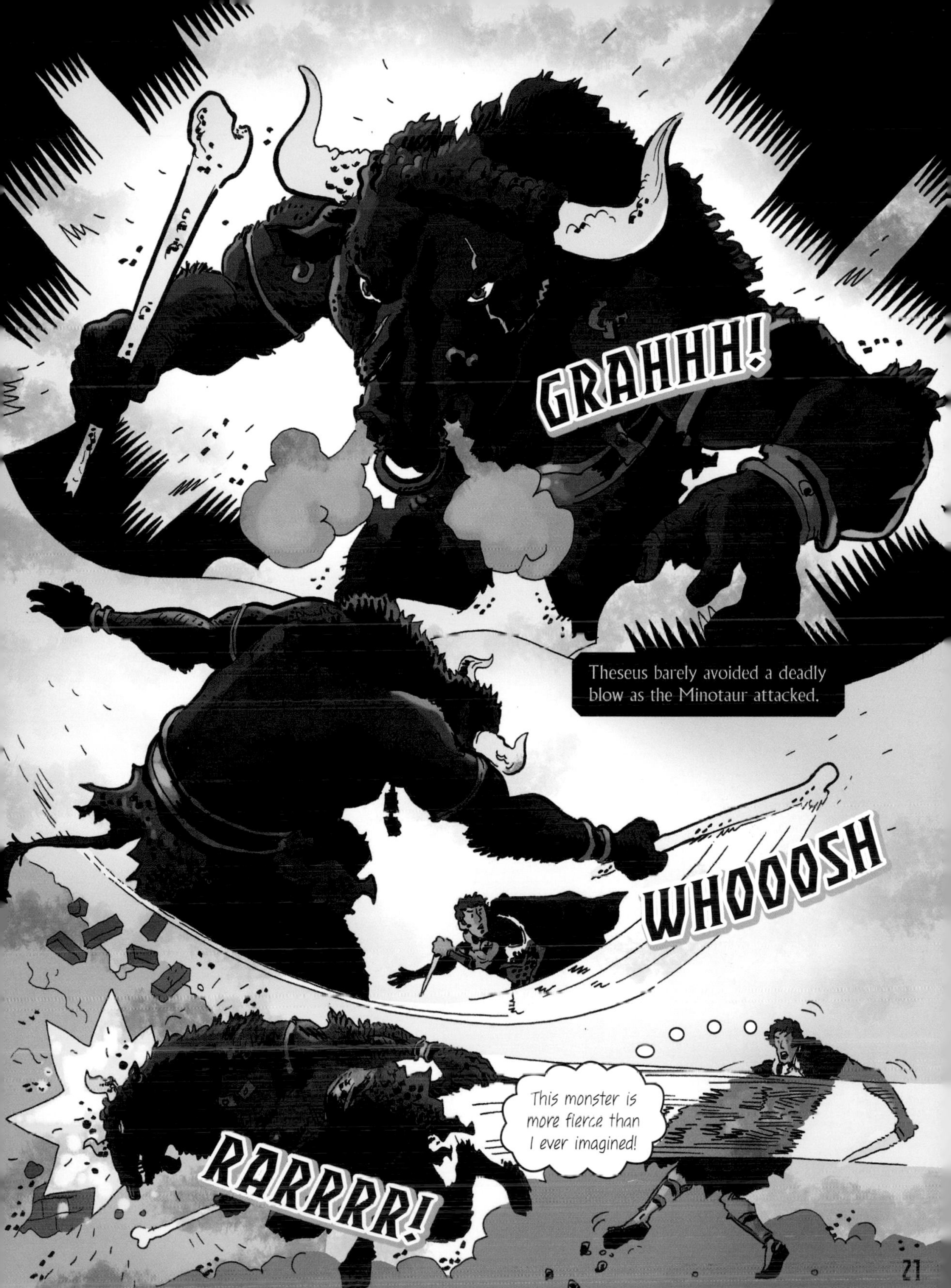
GRAHHH!
Theseus barely avoided a deadly blow as the Minotaur attacked.
WHOOOSH
This monster is more fierce than I ever imagined!
RARRRRR!

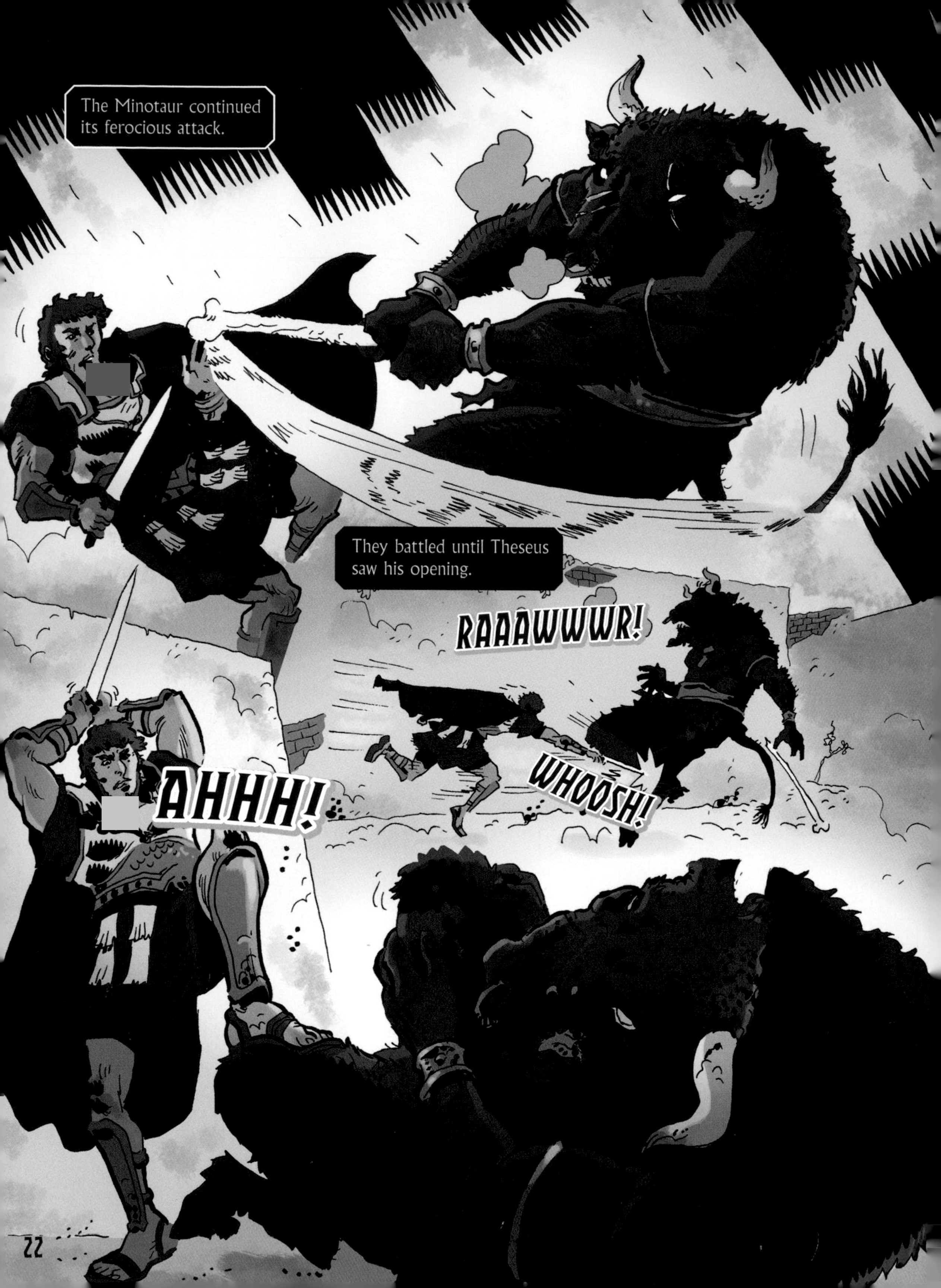
The Minotaur continued its ferocious attack.
They battled until Theseus saw his opening.
RAAAWWWR!
AHHH!
WHOOSH!

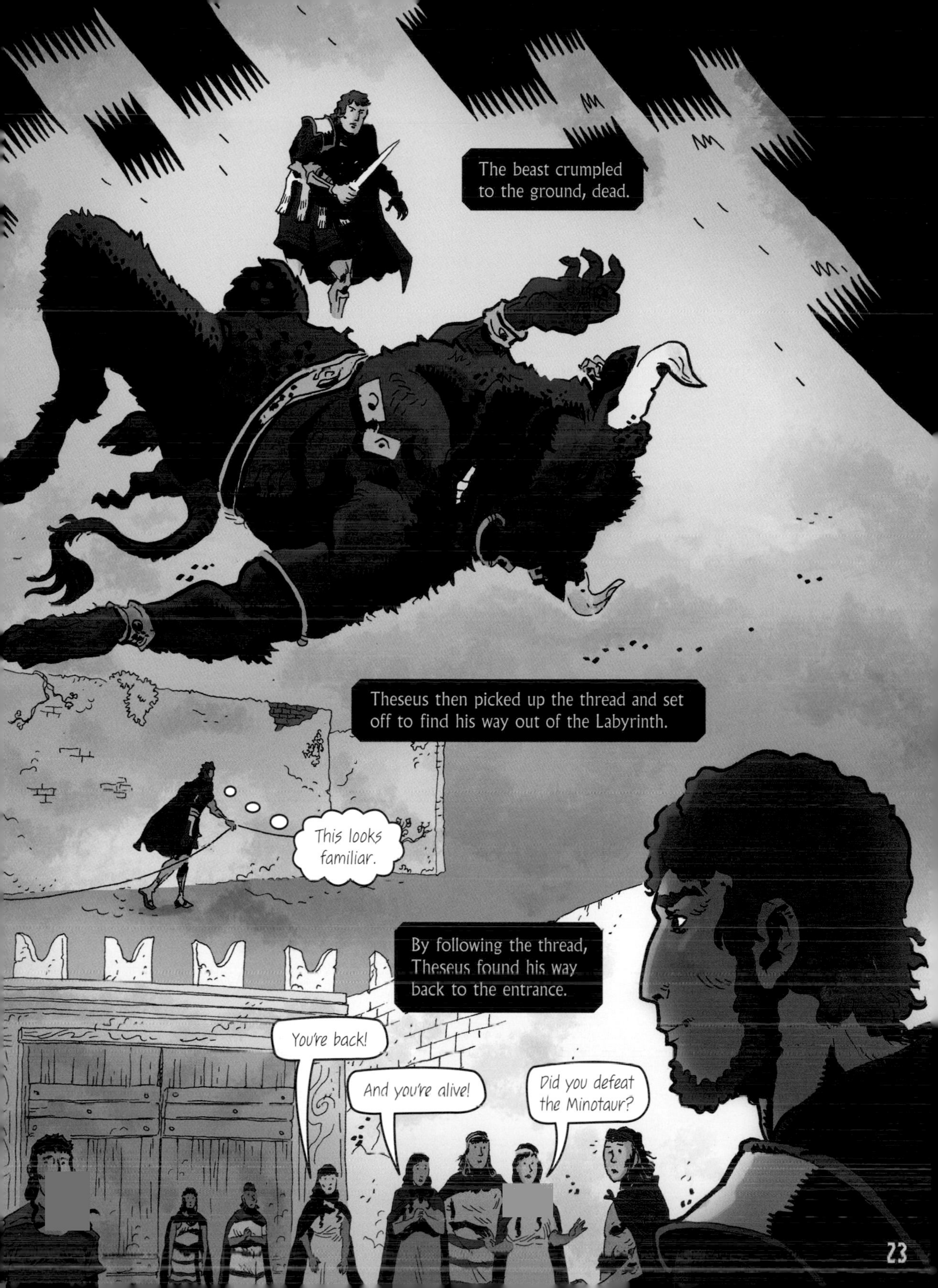
The beast crumpled to the ground, dead.
Theseus then picked up the thread and set off to find his way out of the Labyrinth.
This looks familiar.
By following the thread, Theseus found his way back to the entrance.
You're back!
And you're alive!
Did you defeat the Minotaur?

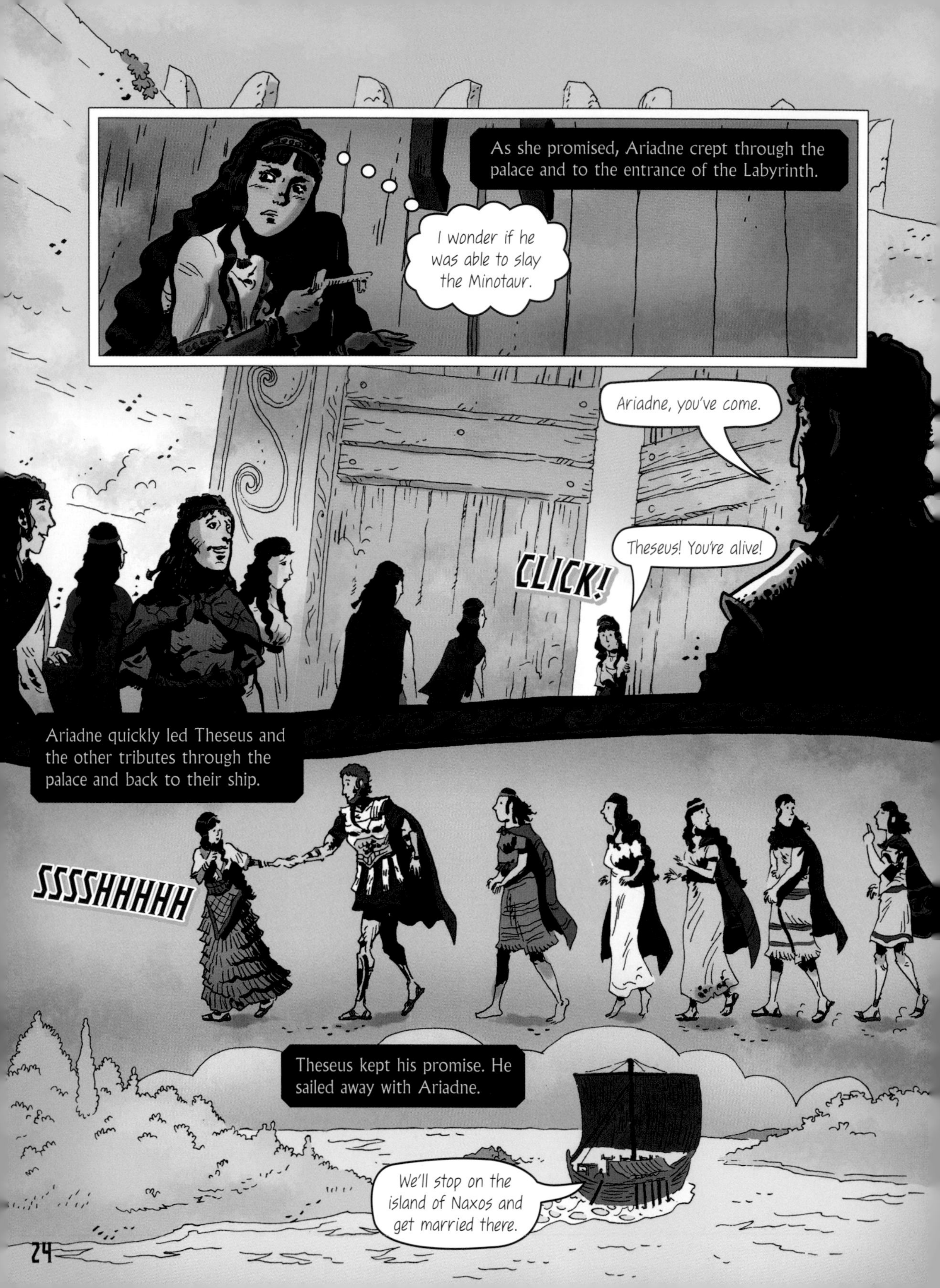
As she promised, Ariadne crept through the palace and to the entrance of the Labyrinth.
I wonder if he was able to slay the Minotaur.
Ariadne, you've come.
Theseus! You're alive!
CLICK!
Ariadne quickly led Theseus and the other tributes through the palace and back to their ship.
SSSSHHHHH
Theseus kept his promise. He sailed away with Ariadne.
We'll stop on the island of Naxos and get married there.

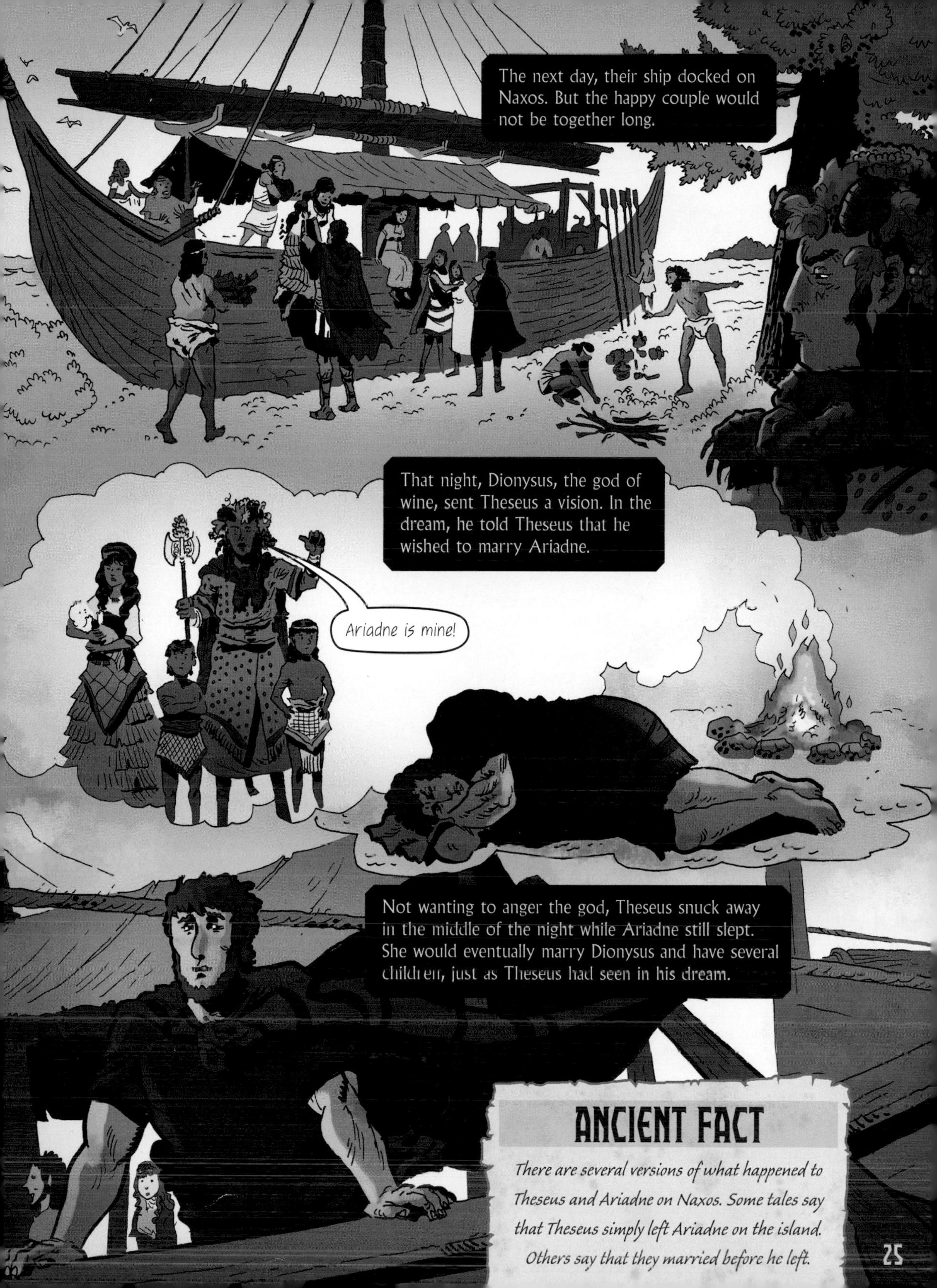
The next day, their ship docked on Naxos. But the happy couple would not be together long.
That night, Dionysus, the god of wine, sent Theseus a vision. In the dream, he told Theseus that he wished to marry Ariadne.
Ariadne is mine!
Not wanting to anger the god, Theseus snuck away in the middle of the night while Ariadne still slept. She would eventually marry Dionysus and have several children, just as Theseus had seen in his dream.

ANCIENT FACT

There are several versions of what happened to Theseus and Ariadne on Naxos. Some tales say that Theseus simply left Ariadne on the island. Others say that they married before he left.

CHAPTER FIVE

THESEUS' LEGACY

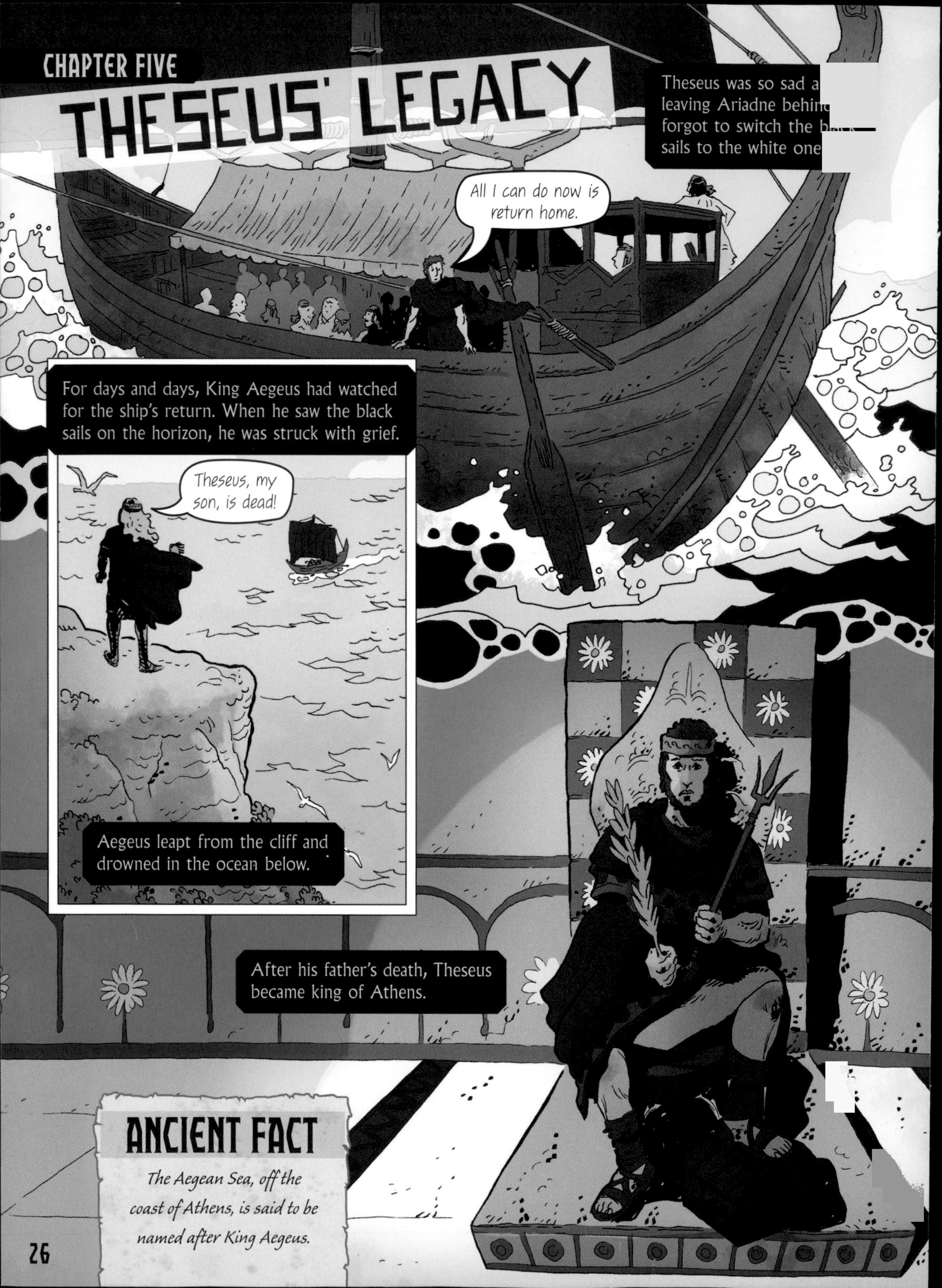
Theseus was so sad a
leaving Ariadne behin
forgot to switch the b
sails to the white one
All I can do now is return home.
For days and days, King Aegeus had watched for the ship's return. When he saw the black sails on the horizon, he was struck with grief.
Theseus, my son, is dead!
Aegeus leapt from the cliff and drowned in the ocean below.
After his father's death, Theseus became king of Athens.

ANCIENT FACT

The Aegean Sea, off the coast of Athens, is said to be named after King Aegeus.

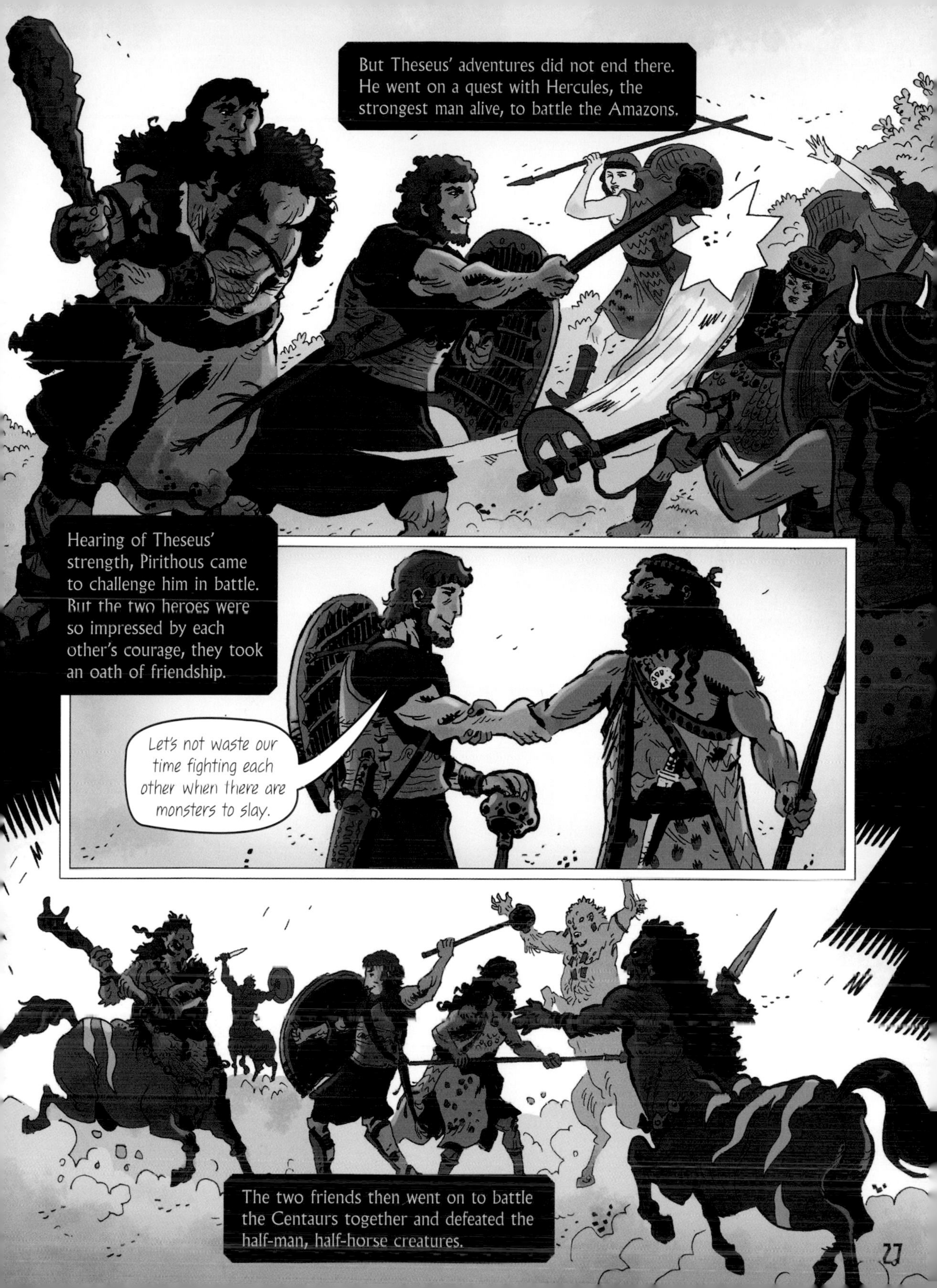
But Theseus' adventures did not end there. He went on a quest with Hercules, the strongest man alive, to battle the Amazons.
Hearing of Theseus' strength, Pirithous came to challenge him in battle. But the two heroes were so impressed by each other's courage, they took an oath of friendship.
Let's not waste our time fighting each other when there are monsters to slay.
The two friends then went on to battle the Centaurs together and defeated the half-man, half-horse creatures.

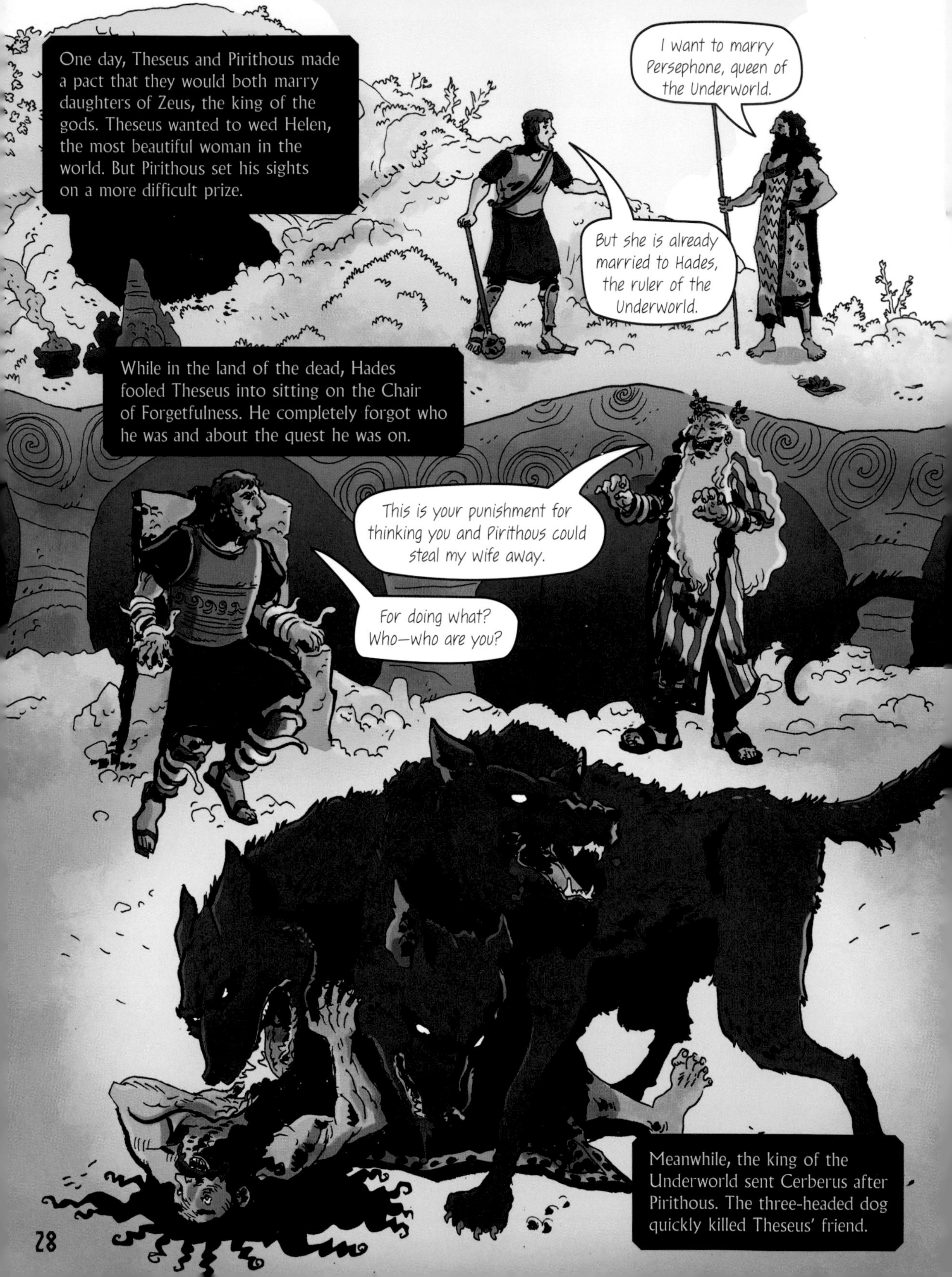
One day, Theseus and Pirithous made a pact that they would both marry daughters of Zeus, the king of the gods. Theseus wanted to wed Helen, the most beautiful woman in the world. But Pirithous set his sights on a more difficult prize.
I want to marry Persephone, queen of the Underworld.
But she is already married to Hades, the ruler of the Underworld.
While in the land of the dead, Hades fooled Theseus into sitting on the Chair of Forgetfulness. He completely forgot who he was and about the quest he was on.
This is your punishment for thinking you and Pirithous could steal my wife away.
For doing what? Who—who are you?
Meanwhile, the king of the Underworld sent Cerberus after Pirithous. The three-headed dog quickly killed Theseus' friend.

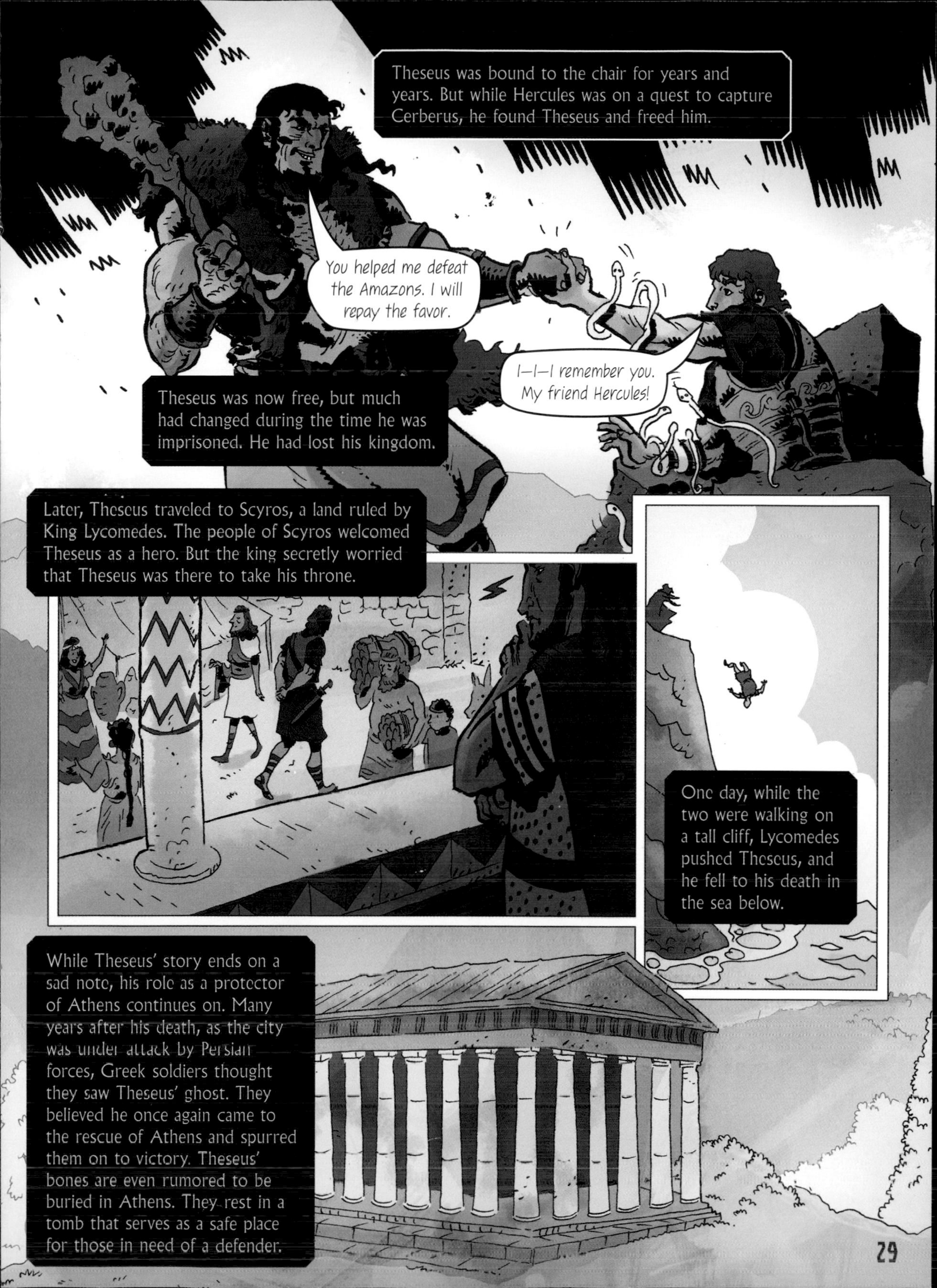
Theseus was bound to the chair for years and years. But while Hercules was on a quest to capture Cerberus, he found Theseus and freed him.
You helped me defeat the Amazons. I will repay the favor.
I—I—I remember you. My friend Hercules!
Theseus was now free, but much had changed during the time he was imprisoned. He had lost his kingdom.
Later, Theseus traveled to Scyros, a land ruled by King Lycomedes. The people of Scyros welcomed Theseus as a hero. But the king secretly worried that Theseus was there to take his throne.
One day, while the two were walking on a tall cliff, Lycomedes pushed Theseus, and he fell to his death in the sea below.
While Theseus' story ends on a sad note, his role as a protector of Athens continues on. Many years after his death, as the city was under attack by Persian forces, Greek soldiers thought they saw Theseus' ghost. They believed he once again came to the rescue of Athens and spurred them on to victory. Theseus' bones are even rumored to be buried in Athens. They rest in a tomb that serves as a safe place for those in need of a defender.

GLOSSARY

expel (IK-spel)—to kick someone out of a place, such as expelling them from a country

goblet (GAH-bleht)—a drinking glass with a stem

labyrinth (LAB-uh-rihnth)—a complex maze

mourning (MORN-ing)—a state of deep sorrow, typically after someone has died

plot (PLAHT)—a plan

quest (KWEST)—a long journey to perform a task or find something

sacred (SAY-krid)—an important religious item

sacrifice (SAK-ruh-feyss)—the act of killing an animal or surrendering a possession as an offering to a god

sorceress (SOR-sur-uhss)—a woman who can perform magic

treachery (TREH-chur-ee)—the betrayal of someone's trust

tribute (TRIH-byoot)—payment made by one ruler or country to another as a sign of dependence

Underworld (UN-dur-wurld)—the land of the dead in myths

READ MORE

Ehrmann, Johanna. *Theseus and the Minotaur.* Jr. Graphic Myths: Greek Heroes. New York: PowerKids Press, 2014.

Hoena, Blake. *Everything Mythology.* National Geographic Kids. Washington, D.C.: National Geographic Children's Books, 2014.

Hunt, Jilly. *Greek Myths and Legends.* Chicago: Capstone Raintree, 2013.

Jeffrey, Gary. *Theseus Battles the Minotaur.* New York: Gareth Stevens Publishing, 2013.

INTERNET SITES

FactHound offers a safe, fun way to find Internet sites related to this book. All of the sites on FactHound have been researched by our staff.

Here's all you do:

Visit *www.facthound.com*

Type in this code: 9781491420751

Super-cool stuff! Check out projects, games and lots more at
www.capstonekids.com

INDEX

TITLES IN THIS SET

A GRAPHIC RETELLING
THE 12 LABORS OF
HERCULES

A GRAPHIC RETELLING
JASON
AND THE ARGONAUTS

A GRAPHIC RETELLING
THE VOYAGE OF
ODYSSEUS

A GRAPHIC RETELLING
THE ADVENTURES OF
PERSEUS

A GRAPHIC RETELLING
THESEUS
AND THE MINOTAUR

A GRAPHIC RETELLING
THE
TROJAN WAR

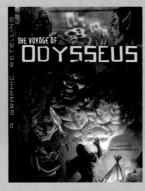

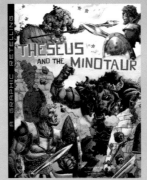